Thoughts, Beliefs, Knowings and Attitudes

by

Michael Cavallaro

Living Concepts LLC
PO Box 374
Red Hill, PA 18076
215-272-3153

For more information please contact:
admin@itstimetoawaken.com
www.itstimetoawaken.com

Acknowledgements

I'd like to thank Nancy Baker and Annmarie Serratore for compiling the material in these books and all the transcribers who made it possible.

Table of Contents

Note from the Author

This is not just another self-help book! This book and others we have written are written so you can have the tools to find your happiness, your soul's purpose and your personal truth. To create an opportunity to eliminate the things that prevent you from accomplishing what you truly desire and from the discovery of who you really are. Simply reading these books will not be enough for your life to change but will however give you the opportunity for great change. Keep in mind that it is up to you to apply this information while developing your own experience and freedom.

These books are not filled with soulful stories, wonderful ideas, and age-old quotes. We are not attempting to tell you we have made a new discovery or found 'THE' answer; only to share with you 'a' way to free yourself from your personal limitations.

Remember: There is nothing new in the universe– only new ways of seeing and experiencing things while being human. Understanding how human life works on multiple levels is part of the preparation to begin living it fully yourself and experiencing, creating and remembering your multidimensional life. Therefore there will be explanations and definitions, all for foundational understanding so that you may begin your own experience of being free from limitations while becoming a conscious divine human.

I want to acknowledge all those in spirit who have guided, directed and suggested the materials that follow as well as my own inner wisdom.

I would also like to acknowledge you and your inner wisdom for taking the time to read this.

Michael Cavallaro

Introduction

Personal growth and enlightenment are much simpler than most people allow them to be. As you read this book keep an open mind and receive the information. Wait to formulate opinions until you have read the entire book. This diverts any judgment which will prevent you from getting as much from this information as possible. In the end it is only your opinion and decision that matters not what this book or any other information may say.

The books we have written are designed to stimulate you to find your own answers within, to give you some guidelines, parameters and tools to help you awaken to your own greatness. These books are intended to provide you with information that may assist you in awakening and in making choices and direction on your journey.

Often times the journey to awakening is perceived to be difficult and challenging. Hopefully these books will assist you in making the road home easier and more comfortable. The tools and concepts are practical and straightforward. The foundation is quite simple, logical, reasonable, rational and most of all practical.

Always remember that any information you come across is

simply that, information. All information that you receive should be felt, understood and discerned carefully to see if it is something that assists you on your journey. Also understand that there is no book or any other form of media that can give you your answers nor can your answers come in one fell swoop or without application of the knowledge you have gained. Knowledge is wonderful but it is not wisdom. Wisdom only comes through experience. If you could understand that all experience leads to wisdom then all of your experiences would be joyful.

For best results with this or any book we've written, read the information, understand it, feel it in your heart, then discern what resonates with you and what is useful for your journey.

Section I

Thoughts, Beliefs, Knowings and More

Thoughts, Beliefs, Knowings and Attitudes

Thought - A process that allows a being to organize or model the world

Belief - An assumed truth

Knowing - More real than a belief; a truth, an unquestionable fact

Attitude - Emotional response to external stimuli based on a judgment

Thoughts

People are more than their thoughts. They are the creators or selectors of their thoughts. Thoughts are acquired through the belief systems that an individual has created or decided to accept as their own and even sometimes are brought into this lifetime with them as a way for their soul to work through certain lessons they have come to complete. These decisions can be made either consciously or unconsciously.

In some cases, beliefs and thoughts are synonymous. Our reference to beliefs is that they are deeper than thoughts and that our thoughts are a result of beliefs. We create beliefs to define our understanding or idea of the world around us and thus, once we have formed a belief, we will find ways to support that belief either consciously or unconsciously. In creating beliefs we have lost "the innocence of a child" and can no longer live in the present moment. Thoughts, attitudes, behaviors and beliefs are the root cause of unhappiness & illness.

As humans we tend to define ourselves and determine our actions by our thoughts, then judge who we are based on these actions. But you are not your thoughts. You select them, either deliberately or not.

Every thought has a frequency. A thought attracts other like frequencies and the same is so for beliefs and knowings. These frequencies form patterns in an individual's energy field. The combination of different thought vibrations creates even more and different patterns that are interwoven so that many thought processes are connected and overlap. This combining of patterns makes life complex and forms a matrix.

The more often the thoughts occur the more likely they are to be long lasting because the more they are repeated the stronger the energetic patterning and the neural pathway in the brain; and the more possibility that they become a belief if they are not already supporting an existing belief.

Part of the difficulty in changing them is the multitude of interwoven patterns from so much energy given to their existence over time. If the thought has turned into a belief it makes it a little more difficult to change.

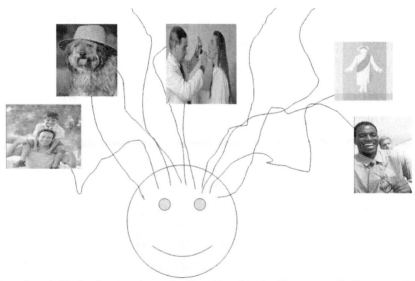

The lines coming out of the head represent unresolved thoughts and worries. They are psychically connected to people, places and things or anything the thought is related to. As long as you think the thoughts whether conscious or not you remain energetically connected. This disperses your energy (energy escapes) and leaves you with the feeling of being spaced out, overwhelmed, unable to focus and not present. When the thought is resolved or stopped the line will disappear leaving more energy for you to focus on the present.

Thoughts, beliefs and knowings affect the etheric, astral, and mental planes, which can be felt on the physical plane by someone who is sensitive. Thoughts are most often formed from the driving force of beliefs. Thoughts create energy patterns that are measurable and can be seen or felt psychically. These are called thought forms. A sensitive or trained person can read thoughts. Thoughts are another form of visualization for those who do not see pictures. After creating desired thought forms, one must focus on them to give them life force or emotional energy so that they may manifest what has been imagined.

Thought frequencies interweave and connect. You may correct one pattern or set of thoughts and later do something that looks like the one you just shifted. All connected patterns (parts of the matrix) or the roots of the patterns must shift for the thinking to shift. Ultimately the belief or knowing behind the thought must change for the process to permanently change. The more often you think the thoughts and the more emotion and feeling put into them, the stronger they are and the more difficult they are to change.

We feel that thoughts are drawn from a pool of existing thoughts that exist in the universe. All thoughts that ever will be thought have already been thought. There are probably no new thoughts just variations on a theme. Every thought that has ever been thought is recorded in the universe (the Akashic records).

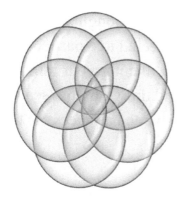

Be careful

what you think-

you just might get it.

Pools of Thoughts

Like thoughts have similar frequencies, they begin as separate things and then join together and form pools. These could be pools of greed, drama, despair, happiness etc. In order for you to think a thought that belongs to a certain pool, you must have beliefs or knowings that have a similar frequency. These pools are also referred to as Energetic Fields of Influence (EFI).

Beliefs are what give you access to the energy fields. Your belief allows you to access that type of thought or gives you the key to a particular pool of thoughts. The more you think the thoughts the more you strengthen and/or support the belief; and the more you remain attached to that energetic field.

You won't have thoughts unless you have a belief that connects you to that energy field because thoughts are what lie in those energy fields. If you are connected to a particular energy field these types of thoughts will enter your mind and you can possibly fall into the pool and drown in that sea of thoughts. For example: someone in shame has access to the pool of shameful thoughts and behaviors.

Because of your vibrational frequency you have limited access to particular beliefs or thoughts and so all the thoughts that ever have been thought, that ever will be thought, that ever can be thought lie in some pools somewhere.

Based upon your vibrational frequency determines what pools you have accessed to. So those pools are kind of like the generation station and you're the generation station on the other end and you hook up with them. Once you hook up with them or connect a cord to them whatever is in in that pool is available to you.

So whatever fits with your belief system along with your energetic frequency comes through that wire. Here are your thoughts. They are not really your thoughts. They aren't really yours they are borrowed thoughts. You are not really the creators of any thoughts; you are the users of thoughts and you can choose to use whatever thoughts you would like to use, but you are not really the creators.

In those pools of frequencies are relative thoughts to those frequencies such as shame, grief, anger, pride, etc. Those pools of thoughts are outside of you. And if you are thinking thoughts and you believe they are yours first, your belief in them has made them yours; you have claimed them. Second, if you are thinking them or ruminating over them, then you have attached to them and focused on them as a reality; and it is a trap of the mind.

I come from the "I can't" pool a whole lot of "I can't" the "I shouldn't" pool, you have a whole lot of "I shouldn'ts" have the "I will but" have a whole lot of "I will but." So what you're not really doing is controlling your thoughts, you're learning to tap into other frequencies at this point. Select the pool you want to play in.

So until you become a creator, you don't create your own thoughts, you borrow thoughts based upon the frequencies you are in. When you become a creator you will have access to all the pools at any given time and will be able to use whatever pool is required for you to use.
So when it is time to use frequency #12 because you need to communicate with frequency #12 people, then you need frequency #343 you will be able to access 343 and talk to people of that frequency.

When not you live in the realm of no thought realm. No thought is the nothingness that they speak of; it is the emptiness they speak of in places. So this is a state but it is not a nothingness state. It is a state of direction.

Direct from the state while you be in the nothingness. While you try to control you cannot be a creator. It is not possible; it is of the mess that control brings that is not even your creation it has just always been always repeating in some other form and some other time from your beliefs and patterns.

Thoughtlessness

Thoughtlessness is a state that is desirable to attain. It is the state of neutrality. In thoughtlessness you can visit any state and not stay in it or be attached to it. In its higher aspect the state of thoughtlessness is pure awareness. Thoughtlessness is to be without thought.

Stop thinking.
Be thoughtless.
If you are thoughtless you are aware.
If you're filled with thought
you are looking for something
in that line of thought.

Thoughtlessness is the state of no thought. In the state of no thought is where peace, joy, enlightenment and real love exist.

If one is in the state of thought there is no room to experience these other things.

Peace, love and joy come from within and so one must be still to notice and experience it. Pleasure comes from outside and one cannot feel inside joy and notice outside pleasure because joy overtakes pleasure.

Energy Patterning of Thoughts and Beliefs

Beliefs and thoughts contain or are made of energy patterns. If focused on enough they create etheric forms. They hover near you or attach to those who vibrate at the same frequency. In so doing they affect the way your life turns out and the way you view life.

You are the creator of these thought forms; therefore to change them you must take ownership and responsibility for them. Because they are invisible and almost never acknowledged, people are not aware of them nor can they even believe they create these things. Some people are not able to conceive of this; so one way to look at it is: it is like lying on a sandy beach all day and not expecting to get sandy or walking in the mud and being surprised you got muddy.

We can relate the energy of beliefs and thoughts to the Energetic Fields of Influence (EFI) and the law of attraction.

> "We can't solve problems by using the same kind of thinking we used when we created them."
> ~ Albert Einstein

Each and every thought, belief and knowing is an energetic pattern. These create the sum total energetic pattern or frequency you live in. In turn, these patterns limit the potential other energetic patterns you may interact with. These may take the form of people, places, things or events. As (the energetic pattern of) dolphins do not live (with the energetic pattern of) horses neither can the energetic pattern of a fearful conservative republican live comfortably with a super liberal democrat nor can a poor person live comfortably with royalty. The frequencies are too different.

Reality

Everything you see comes through your filters or overlays (more about overlays in section III). Have thoughts long enough they become beliefs and attitudes to you because they are assumed to be true.

Everything you see is illusionary fractions and refractions of light; but with your beliefs you make them real. They feel real to you because you are still in them and still believe them. The illusion is your creation and you will get only the answers you (at some level) want whether you are conscious of it or not. That is why nothing outside of you can give the answer or fill the void within. The void within can only be filled with your connection to Source.

When you lack access to another energy field you can't access any thoughts in that energy field. Multiple energy fields have mixes of thoughts with no orderly patterns. Being open to multiple energy fields attracts the belief patterns that match.

Beliefs

Your beliefs are what you are assuming to be true." The core belief of all humans is, "I believe what I believe and/or perceive is real." Everything in your mind is based on a belief or knowing!

Beliefs are for the most part not logical and the more illogical they are, the more guarded they are. Most beliefs are emotionally based and energetically charged. It is the energetic charge that gives them their strength. It is the emotion that gives them their validity.

Thoughts are acquired through belief systems that an individual has created, decided to accept as their own or brought into this lifetime as a way for their soul to work through lessons that it has come to complete.

It is not the belief itself, but the attachment to a belief that makes it yours. This happens in a split second. When you make the belief yours you allow it to unconsciously run your life on autopilot so to speak. Your belief that the beliefs are real is what makes them realities - your realities.

If you could imagine that each belief is like a filter or colored lens and every time you look through it you see things in the different colors of the filter or lens. When you change the lens or change your beliefs you begin to see the world more clearly or differently depending on whether you have eliminated the filters or just simply switched to another filter. Once you accept beliefs as yours, you see the world slightly distorted by these beliefs. Therefore changing your beliefs changes your realities and what you see.

> *Your beliefs in the beliefs*
> *makes them real to you.*

You are not your beliefs; you are the creator of them. When you become a conscious observer it gives you the ability to detach from your beliefs for a moment to decide which beliefs serve you and which ones do not. Then after a while you can become a decider of behaviors and actions that were based upon the original beliefs but now are simply actions or behaviors you use in the world; thereby giving you the ability to see where they do not serve you and then to change them. This simply means that you no longer believe your beliefs, but you can use the behaviors that you learned while having your beliefs as tools to integrate with the world and interface with other human beings.

You are not created by your beliefs.

You are the creator of them.

Scientifically it has been proven that thoughts are energy. They actually carry what is called neurological weight that can be measured, and this can affect the neural-chemical balance in a person's brain. Again, more physical evidence of what we've said earlier. By changing your beliefs you change your thoughts and your thoughts change the normal chemical balance in your body and your brain. Thus, you change the way you feel and also change the way you see the world.

Balloon Metaphor

You can make a little analogy and you could say, "Imagine that your consciousness is a hot air balloon; that all of your beliefs are sandbags, and your consciousness wants to rise. So what do you have to do to rise?" Metaphorically, "Raising the balloon" means raising your frequencies to a higher vibration. And just like in a hot air balloon, the higher you get up, the more you can see, the greater your vision and you are fully present in the basket of that hot air balloon. Otherwise, you crash and burn.

So every belief is a sandbag. And the more belief systems that you can get rid of, so to speak, the more bags you are dropping off of your basket which allows your balloon or your consciousness to rise a little bit further. The more you do faster, the quicker you rise. If you do it too fast, then your balloon goes into such a high altitude that you may lose consciousness again. And at this point, it is your human that is losing consciousness because your pure consciousness cannot be lost. But your human awareness of it can if it rises too fast. It will short out your human programs. It will blow the circuitry.

So by taking off the bags as fast as you can it allows you to rise as fast as you can. But if you just cut them all off and your balloon sailed straight up, that would be like dropping the body; it would be like ascending without the body, without your human consciousness.

The choice is yours. You can remain in these patterned beliefs that you have assumed to be truths or you can seek and become aware of what is the truth and then choose the behaviors your wish to use while interfacing with the world.

What do you really believe?
More than you are aware of!

How Beliefs Are Created

Beliefs come from our own experience; either from this lifetime, another life experience (assuming "past lives"), or as an unquestioned acceptance of what other people say or do. The majority of beliefs are created at a young age, usually by 6 to 8 years of age. From this point on, very few new beliefs are created. The new ones that are created usually occur as a result of perceived traumatic or very intense experiences.

As young children, we make sense of the world by creating beliefs (or assuming truths) about ourselves, our parents, other people, and almost everything else around us. We are like sponges, absorbing new information from all around—this helps us to understand the world and create order from the mountains of information being thrown at us. These beliefs create our realities.

The majority of beliefs are chosen unconsciously or semiconsciously. Unconscious decisions about accepting or creating beliefs occur when, particularly as a child, you have watched something that is being done or how people interact and you have decided that this is the way you will act without even knowing it. Semi-conscious decisions to create beliefs are when you see something done or said and you think to yourself, even though briefly, "This will work for me, I will do this."

Ultimately your beliefs are your imaginary creations.

For example: A child watches his dad yelling at and berating his mom. The child notices that mom stops what she is doing to focus on dad. Later, the child asks mom to play with him, but she is too busy. So he yells at her like he saw dad do. Mom immediately stops what she's doing to pay attention to him.

As a result, the child creates a belief that if he yells, mom (or women) will pay attention to him.

Children may fight the beliefs and/or behaviors they acquire because they dislike them. They may want to be different. But to no avail, as these have already become beliefs. They may try to do something different but with no training or modeling on how to alter the beliefs, the child is at the mercy of their current belief system and destined to live the way the generations before them have, believing, "This is just the way it is."

Another example: A child's parents are prejudice against another race. So the child sees, hears and feels this. She comes of age and goes to school and happens to like another child of a different race. She is now conflicted as to how she should behave.

She may be both nice and mean to this other child but when this new "friend" does something she does not like she begins to use racial slurs and mean statements. Now she appears prejudice when in fact she was only mad.

The parents reinforce the racial prejudice, the child assumes they are correct and bonds with racism due to her hurt and anger. The child grows up assuming she is racist while still liking people of different races. This creates a conflict within between family loyalty, personal identity, emotions and other human beings.

As you can see the assumed truths, beliefs and misperceptions create great hardships in the human arena. This is just one small example of what occurs every day in so many ways. Beliefs that were never questioned become a way of life.

> ### *Believing in beliefs is not necessary.*

These beliefs are accepted as fact or truth. As people move through life they tend to believe and assume everything they experience that is related to or looks and feels like the original source of that belief is the same. When this occurs the automatic response to those beliefs becomes evident in their behaviors and reactions. As these beliefs begin to grow in momentum and strength, a person develops behaviors to support them.

Life experiences chosen by your soul

or spirit are also a factor.

If you come into this life needing to resolve the belief that people who love you hurt you, you may be born into a family that has these same beliefs or reinforce them. Later in life you will most likely find someone to love who will hurt you or who you will believe is hurting you. This then reinforces: "Those who love you hurt you." when in truth the other person may have had no intention of hurting you.

This is often mistakenly called self-sabotage or self-fulfilling prophecy. In truth it is simply a belief system creating the reality it is designed to create. As you test out these behaviors with different people and in different situations, you begin to form a belief system based on what you learn.

Continuing with a previous example: the child begins to form more beliefs as he continue to test his behaviors and the responses he receives. If he yells at dad, dad may punish him. So the child forms a belief that men in authority positions punish you for yelling. If the child doesn't yell in class one day and doesn't get the attention he wants from his classmates, he forms another belief that he has to yell to get his classmates to pay attention to him. The result of all these beliefs is the creation of a belief system about yelling and ultimately a way of life.

The collective result of these behaviors and beliefs is a pattern. A pattern is a set of unconscious and often automatic behaviors that stem from a belief or belief system. In the example previously used, the child's pattern becomes yelling when he wants attention. This pattern is now ingrained in him. He begins to act upon it unconsciously whenever he feels like he is being ignored or not getting the attention he wants. As he grows up, this pattern stays with him and in fact gets stronger and more automatic.

As an adult at work, he gets into constant arguments with coworkers when things don't go the way he planned. He also constantly butts heads with female supervisors though never challenges his male bosses. He can't understand why women are so argumentative or why he is always arguing with his coworkers. He is not aware that he is stuck in a pattern. It has become a frustrating way of life. Life seems so hard and now possibly depression or some other challenge sets in.

Human Model of the World

The basic human model of the world and the way every human operates is:

- My beliefs support, create and justify my perceptions.
- My perceptions create my reality.
- My reality determines my behaviors which creates a magnetic energetic field that attracts and determines the way the world shows up around me.
- The way it shows up around me justifies and supports my beliefs.

Common Human Beliefs

To understand the human belief systems we will create a basic outline. This outline we will call the human belief system. In the human belief systems, simplistically we would say there are four categories:

- **Personal beliefs**: These beliefs create total separation and are completely self-centered, where the individual is the center of the universe.

- **Familial beliefs**: We create a separation of small groups that are blood related and the family is the center of the universe.

- **Cultural beliefs**: These create separation into larger groups with an understanding that we are special because we are this group. This is where country or race is the center of the universe.

- **Human beliefs**: These separate us into one large group, into human beings separate from all else into the universe, where human beings are the center of the universe.

All beliefs are self-created. They are created by the choices we make about accepting things as our truth or not. Even if we are not conscious of our choices they are still choices.

Evidence of them being our choice is the fact that siblings having the same parents turn out differently. Each sibling chooses different events to accept and perceive as "truth." If this was not so, then all siblings would see the world the same and have the exact same beliefs. Without choice, all people from the same family would be and feel the same. Even identical twins have different ways of seeing the word.

Beliefs are the foundation of your human experience.

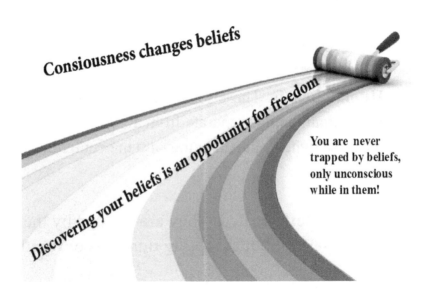

Consiousness changes beliefs

Discovering your beliefs is an oppotunity for freedom

You are never trapped by beliefs, only unconscious while in them!

Beliefs are for the most part not logical and the more illogical they are, the more guarded they are. For the most part beliefs are emotionally based and energetically charged. It is the energetic charge that gives them their strength. It is the emotion that gives them their validity. We tend to believe that things will happen as they have always happened.

Emotions are not real; they are merely a result of another belief system.
If they were real, everyone on the planet would feel the same about everything.

Believing our Beliefs

There is currently a theory that you attract things into your life and these things come toward you. We would suggest here that because of your beliefs you resonate with a certain frequency and because of that frequency you are more likely to enter into environments that will support your current belief system. It is not that you are a victim of circumstance and things just come toward you because you believe things. It is more that because you resonate at a certain frequency you tend to enter into environments of your choosing.

There cannot be a thought without a belief system to support it. The original attachment to an original event creates a belief; then the attachment to that belief is what makes it yours.

These 'truths' are never challenged because they are assumed true even if they are false. Most of us are willing to look at all aspects of our lives except our beliefs. Notice that when people become defensive it is when their beliefs are challenged. Why? Because our beliefs are the foundation on which our ego is based and if they are wrong we are wrong. When beliefs are challenged the ego is threatened and it must protect itself.

It is important to remember that we are not our beliefs; we are the creators of them. We can be conscious observers of them thereby giving us the ability to see where they do not serve us and begin to change them.

Beliefs beget their own multiple realities so that when you attempt to change them you are still caught in them and the belief that they are real.

Example:
>*-The belief that you are trying to get out of a belief, leads to:*
>>*-The belief that the belief is real, which leads to,*
>>>*-The belief that you are stuck in the belief, which leads to,*
>>>>*-The belief that I am in the belief, which leads to,*

-The belief I must rid myself of this belief, which leads to,
    -The belief that the belief is real and so on it goes.

The belief

"I am in the belief."

Keeps you in the belief!

All parts of your life and programs support this patterning, which is an attempt of the unconscious to maintain its program. The many different beliefs look different, but they all have the same goal – maintain the current belief system. The beliefs also fool you by getting you to think the belief is "over there" or about something or someone other than you. By falling for this misperception you do not realize it is in you! Therefore you do not notice it is running your life while it keeps you in the loop.

Judging the belief is an unconscious admission that the belief is real and that you have to "do" something to deal with or combat it. Nothing could be more inaccurate. *Judging your beliefs creates an emotional and mental attachment to them.* Once you have created this attachment these beliefs and/or experiences have become yours!

Beliefs eventually turn into belief systems. A belief system is often a complex design of multiple beliefs creating an entire system. This belief system could be completely self-created or adapted from a family belief system or cultural belief system. Within each person's belief system there are often unique variations to the cultural or family belief system. Belief systems are like opinions, everyone has one. However, just because you have one does not mean it is necessarily accurate or that it serves you well. This is why you must question everything and then discern and decide if it is for you.

At some level, life itself is actually a belief system. Because of this you can actually create any type of life you wish. Becoming aware of your beliefs and belief systems frees you from their limitations. By having this freedom you may then re-create a new conscious perspective on how you wish to perceive life. This then creates a new vibratory frequency which allows you to become a creator rather than a victim to your beliefs and belief systems.

Your new beliefs are based upon your intent. You may intend to ignore truth and fact and create a fantasy reality or you can see things as they truly are. By seeing and interpreting life clearly you can actually create the life that you want while dismantling the old beliefs that no longer serve you. You may also choose to believe that you cannot do what we have just explained. It's all up to you, you can have what you want and you can have it all! *What do you believe?*

Holding onto Beliefs

Life is simple once you understand how it works!

To experience the simplicity you must make conscious choices.

People will hold onto their beliefs as long as they believe those beliefs serve them. So as long as I am fearful of something ever occurring to myself or anyone in the world, I will retain that belief. When I am finished being fearful of this occurrence or finished with my pain, I will then decide that, "Oh, I can release this now."

When I recognize and see that my fear and my experience is no longer possible today with the consciousness that I have and I no longer live in the past, then I am free to release the belief and see the experience as benign. But as long as I carry the pain and chose to hold onto the pain because maybe I need to remember; because maybe I need to remain afraid so that I am on guard; maybe I need to remind others about the terrible pain they might have because I had it when I was little, in the past, some other time; as long as I retain that I, will maintain that belief.

But when I realize that the past is no longer relevant to my present experience and I want to live wholly and fully in the moment, I will then say, "Oh, it is time for me to see this differently." And hence the concept from The 55 Concepts, "Everyone is ready in their own time."

Types of Beliefs

Core Beliefs - Beliefs that are never questioned become core beliefs because you accepted them at your core. Usually they are the ones that create long term damage or challenges in your life. You will tend to repeat the same stuff, run into the same problems even though you intellectually know better. Usually people do not look deep within themselves to understand why these things are happening.

The truth about core beliefs is that all human beings use these as the foundation for their life on earth and their behavior until some form of desire for greater consciousness takes place. Core beliefs often have created or spawned other beliefs. Often these beliefs as well must be cleared or they regrow a version of the original belief.

These beliefs are almost never questioned when things don't work; and because of them external circumstances are often blamed. If there is questioning it is usually about how circumstances or people have caused you to do what you have done. there is very little teaching about how your beliefs create your reality, so therefore people rarely know what to do or how to permanently change.

Because of this, core beliefs are never questioned. Therefore associated experiences and behaviors are continually repeated during life. The most challenging and difficult beliefs are very subtle because there is never a great enough emotional stir. The belief only provides you with a sense of knowing or expectation which is not reality based but belief based. This makes it almost impossible to discern what is causing the challenges.

Core beliefs give one a sense of identity. They are 'who I am' statements. To remove or alter these core beliefs often brings about great inexplicable fear. If this happens to you know that it is a loss of identity and the ego personality is in danger of losing its control over your life. This is actually a very positive

sign, although it feels unpleasant. It will feel like you are going to die, yet there is no immediate or apparent danger.

At this point those not fully committed to their growth will get busy, stop or avoid growth work, channel their pattern into something else or anything the ego personality can do to preserve the old way. Do not give in to the fear and panic. Remain consistent and continue your growth. Be patient; it will pass. It is change on a deep level. You will not die! Core beliefs are close to knowings. Most core beliefs are about your present life.

Core beliefs may be unquestioned beliefs and/or experiential beliefs, or some combination thereof. These are always then emotional and mentally cemented in. Some core beliefs are: "I am my body." "I am my beliefs." "I am human." "I believe my beliefs."

Experiential Beliefs - These beliefs are beliefs formed through experience. "I have seen it, done it, felt it therefore it must be true." is the rationale behind these types of beliefs. These are often the beliefs of the entrepreneur, artist and freethinker. These beliefs are very difficult to change for those who create and accept their beliefs this way. Simply because the beliefs usually must be changed through a new experience; which may be a long wait or process.

People who use their experience as a foundation for their beliefs usually are more adventurous. They tend to distrust authority, prefer to find out for themselves and are not as easily influenced by others. Authorities or experts are not blindly trusted just because of their position or title or for their knowledge. Knowledge is not wisdom and can be inaccurate. They will only trust someone or something if their experience dictates an acceptable truth. For these people it is experience that determines trust. These people tend to be the independent entrepreneur type. They usually have to "find out" and then make their own choice if it suits them. Credentials and titles are irrelevant. The proven experienced person is more reliable than a degree or letters behind a name.

The problem with these types of beliefs is that you may set yourself up for an experience that supports the belief without even knowing it. By being unconscious of this you continually believe and experience the truth of any given belief. Even though these experiences are self-created, it is perceived by the believer that these are real, true and factual, when in truth they are not.

Experiential beliefs are an experience that is seated emotionally and then mentally cemented in. Some examples of experiential beliefs are:

- Putting your hand on a burner burns.
- Knowing someone will hurt you – they do and you can expect it.

- If I tell the truth I'll get punished – and I do.

Assumed Beliefs - People who assumingly accept other people's opinions and deeds as their foundation tend to be more cautious. They tend to be more trusting at first, as well as accepting of authority and experts. These people are usually followers. Authorities are people trusted because of their perceived power and position. Experts are trusted for their perceived knowledge. They love credentials as a proof of someone's wisdom. This allows them to avoid their own self-discovery, fear of failure and the unknown. It is consciously or unconsciously seen as the safe way. These people tend to believe first and are disappointed if what they accepted was incorrect. After many disappointments they often become untrusting of others. They begin very naive and gullible then after life experience hits them they often become cynical.

> **Are your beliefs really yours**
>
> **or have you just assumed they were yours?**

Which is yours?

Everyone has one or the other of the two processes above as a foundation and some combination of both as a secondary process. The assuming person often thinks their cynicism is the same as that of the experiential person. It looks similar but is driven by a different need.

When you are seeking to change beliefs, find out where you get your beliefs. If you tend towards self-generated beliefs then use experiences or rational approaches. If your beliefs are more external, then expert or authority information will help. But to bring about real, permanent change, you must eventually switch to the process of self-generation and self-discovery. Anything less always has a greater margin of error and still is not yours, though if you manifested it, it's yours!

Unquestioned Beliefs

An unquestioned belief is a 100% assumed truth, no proof, no experience. These beliefs are usually obtained through observation and energetically assimilated from cultural and familial environments. These beliefs may also be a soul memory brought in with an individual to resolve.

These beliefs are generally formed in childhood for the following reasons:
- a child has limited perceptions

- the child is vulnerable due to their dependence on their caretakers or parents
- a child has limited abilities to validate or verify information

- a child typically uses their parents or caretaker as a basis for their own identity

Typically unquestioned thoughts and beliefs that are not challenged by a group or individual (family, society, religion etc.) become group truths or beliefs. They often appear as the beliefs of the fanatic or the zealot. There is blind commitment to fulfill the belief at any cost, without rational thought, fact, reason or logic.

Example: In many cultures it is acceptable to kill, eliminate or discriminate against people with different beliefs or ideas. It is common for one political or religious group to respond towards another political or religious group in these ways without question.

Unquestioned individual beliefs lead to the person following the family patterns and repeating the same errors and mistakes in life. These same errors and mistakes may take on a different appearance due to circumstances but the essence of these are the same.

Question Everything!
Especially that which you
have never questioned!

Unquestioned beliefs are strong and never challenged by the believer. If someone else challenges these unquestioned beliefs, the believer will instinctively fight against the challenge without thought or investigation. The believer is almost always in the state of low self-esteem, lack of individual identity, and driven by the need to believe something, have value or somehow support another belief.

Example: Frank believes that he should die for his country. However Frank has never looked into the reason that his country is at war and the validity of its claims. If Frank would look closely he would find out that his country's claims are mostly false and are being used to take over another country's economy. If Frank were to discover this he may lose faith in

The believer of beliefs is always disconnected from their own spirit.

his country and would come to the feeling that he doesn't belong there. With this new feeling he would not know where to go or to take his family. So Frank consciously chooses not to research the truth and would rather die for his country. This gives him value and worth based upon the design of values in his particular culture.

Unquestioned beliefs are assumed and then mentally cemented in with emotion. This formula creates a very loyal and easily manipulated human being. This is a type of brainwashing often used by governments, militaries, religions and cults as a way to maintain and control a select group of peoples.

Example: Mary believes in the church and Jesus Christ. She goes to church regularly and donates time and money to the church and its claimed cause (assumed belief). The church tells Mary that she will go to heaven (assumed belief) if she does these deeds and sacrifices herself (mental/ emotion).

Due to these two factors when Mary finds out about the priests sexually abusing children she ignores the fact that the church refuses to do anything about it and has been shuffling priests from parish to parish for years.

Ignoring what is happening allows Mary to still feel like what she belongs to is infallible and that she is going to heaven because that's what the infallible church tells her and it also allows the church to continue these abusively accepted policies.

Consciously Self-Serving Beliefs

Consciously self-serving beliefs are created to justify desires or other beliefs. These beliefs are usually emotional with a dash of mental cement. They are used to manipulate others and the environment. They are also used to support and hide other fearful, uncertain beliefs or desires. These beliefs are often readily defended like unquestioned beliefs. They are defended out of fear rather than commitment. Defense of beliefs may take place internally as well as externally. Disbelief is a form of defense to preserve existing beliefs. These beliefs usually justify their existence with an explanation of why they exist and why they must be kept.

Exercise: Write down the beliefs you hold that have never questioned or that you hold without truth or fact to support them. Things you are just doing because you were told to do them. Write why you do them.
Then write why you behave or how you believe you are supposed to behave or be as a person. Why you believe that and what proof you have to support being that way. Ultimately you are questioning your foundational beliefs in order to free you from these structures.

Beliefs and Language

> *Be aware of how you are feeling when you speak*
>
> *in order to avoid creating things*
>
> *you do not really want or intend*

Our understanding of the world is determined by the language we use. In effect, we speak reality into existence. Language is a pattern of frequencies used to convey experience. Patterns are used to make a common reality understood. Understanding is the basis of human communication. Beliefs limit communication.

Beliefs are built into language and language is used to express beliefs. Language is designed to communicate experience, so people try to verbalize their beliefs and perceptions of those beliefs. When we use language and put a word to something, we label it. If we label it with a word, it is "real", we believe it exists. Once something is labeled we limit it. Placing a word on something is to energetically put it in a box or contain it. From this beliefs are born and continually confirmed. This is a form of self-brainwashing.

Different cultures express their beliefs with different patterns. So if you are used to a particular pattern (language), then when you go to another culture or country you may not understand their pattern of expressing beliefs (language). Beliefs are generally the same around the world; it is only the way they are patterned differently and the way patterns are verbalized that are different. Humans are humans. We all operate the same. We are only patterned differently therefore we communicate differently.

You choose your words with a purpose whether you know it or not. This becomes all the more important to realize as you become conscious. When you are conscious a different set of rules apply to this game: the energy and intent of your words create. They are not just empty words, they are filled with energy. As you grow you really must be aware of what you say, how you say it and why it is being said. A less conscious person will tell you their beliefs through their words; how they see the world, but their words do not have the same power and effect as those of a conscious person who has that different energy.

As you speak you reinforce the beliefs you have. Other people psychically respond to the energy or vibration of your words. Beware of the negative attitudes you portray and reinforce with the words you use. Be careful of your words!

The spoken word is MAGIC.

The spoken word creates and destroys without effort and often unnoticed. What is actually spoken is also often combined with intention and non-verbal communication. The feeling and invisible message conveyed through the spoken word is often more important than the words themselves. As words are spoken there is a frequency that is transmitted, this is why words are so powerful.

The Major Problem with Beliefs

You tend to believe that things will happen according to what you think and/or believe. This puts you in the position of perceiving present events through the filters of your past. This prevents you from experiencing the "now." You can never be fully present or experience something truly new if you are perceiving life through your beliefs from the past. In other words your previous beliefs limit your present experience.

Belief Support - Once we have established a belief, it is the job of our unconscious to support it and either create or perceive an environment that supports the belief. The ego also must support and defend it. If confronted by another's belief, the ego will try to discredit their challenges and prove its own beliefs. The more a belief is integrated into the entire matrix of beliefs, the more difficult and dangerous it is for the ego to let go of it. The removal of one belief now threatens other beliefs. Therefore many beliefs are going to protect themselves and the defenses will become stronger and more intense.

For example: If you believe, "Other people judge me." No matter what anybody says you will find negativity in their statement to prove they are judging you. You will also be critical of others and judge them; thereby keeping yourself in the energy of being judged.

In order to change beliefs you must clear the energy charge from the mind, the brain (neural pathways) and emotions. The energy of the belief creates its own neural pathways, so that every time you get in that energy field or sensate experience it will use and access those neural pathways. Changes MUST take place in a person's belief system, thought process, the brain energetically, the brain's patterning, the mental, emotional, causal bodies and soul memory for change to be permanent.

Can you change your own beliefs? Yes but not without some assistance. Typically people just don't decide to believe differently and then do. Fortunately or unfortunately:

People believe what they believe.

People and History Repeat Themselves

People repeat the beliefs, thoughts and behaviors they are exposed to as children whether it is apparent or not. People select the behaviors consciously and unconsciously that they are exposed to that serve their personality and soul purpose needs.

People would like to believe they are more conscious than they actually are. The truth is when it comes to beliefs and behaviors people are repeaters, copiers and modifiers. Unless they consciously make the changes and make the effort to change their conscious and unconscious beliefs there is no true originality or changing history.

History repeats itself because people as a whole do not fundamentally change. What this means is that people do not take the time to re-pattern their beliefs so even though they may have a mental understanding of what is not working they commonly fall back into their patterned belief systems. Yet even with this knowledge they typically relive their history in a different time and place with different people and circumstances but with the same driving issues as in the past.

History goes something like this: There is a perceived injustice, then there is an argument, then a fight or a war, then a winner and loser, then if they are lucky an understanding or agreement. This then is followed by a healing of the wounds, then comfort, then habit, then status quo. At this point the old patterns typically resurface. This occurs almost out of an unconscious boredom, they see a perceived injustice, then an argument begins, then a fight or war, then… and so it goes – and there you have, history!

If people can't even resolve family and personal patterning, how can they resolve cultural or national patterning? If this can't be done, then how can there be world peace? It all begins and ends with each individual ending the conscious or unconscious war within.

All Beliefs Should Be Questioned

No matter how sure you are: question everything! Especially those things you've never questioned! By questioning you can find the source. Pay attention to evidence. Avoid skipping past what you see just because you have already concluded or believe something. Once the belief is looked at carefully and fully evaluated you can then make a conscious decision in regards to that belief. Fear of or the resistance to questioning a belief is a sign that there is a falsehood somewhere within the belief system or that you are choosing to hide something. Your job is to question with curiosity, inquisitiveness and the, openness of a child – pure in nature. The absolute truth will always withstand any amount of observation and questioning.

Knowings

When we speak of knowings here, we are speaking of first level or human knowings, those that contain our beliefs. We will speak of a deeper level of knowings later.

Knowings are a combination of core beliefs, unquestioned beliefs, the human system of beliefs and soul memory. What most people call core beliefs are much more than they currently understand.

Because these knowings are so deeply embedded in the human belief system they are much more powerful than any individual beliefs. This is due to the sheer volume of energy as you are dealing with a group or mass consciousness of billions of people. The more people who share a belief the stronger that belief is and the more it becomes an assumed limitation. An unquestioned belief, core belief and human belief together make it more intensely real because it is a "group effort".

Knowings are beyond beliefs. We see them as unquestionable fact. Technically, they are the deepest of beliefs inherent in humans. They are so deep, so subtle, people can't even conceive of them as beliefs or even the possibility of questioning them.

Examples of such beliefs are: rocks are hard, bodies are real, what I believe or perceive really exists, I am separate from God, what I see or feel is real, walls are solid, I must eat to live, etc.

"If I know it then it is." "If it has been then it will always be." are the premise of a knowing; it is to not be challenged and never is. You just know!

Everything you know isn't what it seems!

Once a knowing is challenged it becomes an opportunity to expand your consciousness.

> **Just because you know something now, does it mean**
> **it will always be so?**
> **Didn't humans once know the world was flat?**
> **Didn't humans once believe they could not fly?**
> **Is anything known truly real or is there a truth**
> **beyond what is known?**

With questions there are often doubts. Doubts are the result of beliefs or knowings about to be surpassed. Surpassing old beliefs or knowings often creates fear for the ego personality. However, becoming more conscious allows you to go beyond beliefs and knowings to access the wisdom of your own soul/spirit.

Doubt about what can be done is only doubt about what you will do. Remember: question everything!

Are you absolutely sure:

The earth is solid?
Water is wet?
You are the center of the universe?
You are separate from God and others?
What you perceive is real?
Your truth is the real truth?
Everyone thinks like you?
Everyone does the things you do for the same reason (stories)?

Connected awareness of and to your own inner spirit replaces thoughts, beliefs and knowings.

Attitudes

Along with thoughts, beliefs and knowings let's clearly add attitudes. Attitudes are the emotional component of this experience. Attitudes are the emotions or emotional energy that support or go along with your thoughts, beliefs and knowings.

Attitudes here are slightly different than what you heard growing up when you were told about 'your attitude' but they are yet similar.

Some attitudes you may have heard about: "Don't have that attitude with me." "You have a poor attitude." or "That is a great attitude." These were basically people telling you that they liked or didn't like the emotion or feeling that they were feeling coming from you. Often this is then interpreted as: "I am or am not acceptable."

There was a misinterpretation that what other people did or did not like feeling was your fault. This feeling was then often associated with a behavior, which then lead to the belief that you were those behaviors, which lead to an identity associated to that set of behaviors. This created the belief in a false identity you assumed to be you!

So understand:

**When someone does not like your attitude
they do not like the way they feel you feeling.**

Attitudes are conveyed through feeling and the sensate body. Because attitudes are a feeling, they can often not be described. Attitudes are a feeling sense of how you are inside, how you are being, how you appear, it is all about the feeling. It is all about the sensate body.

The sensate body is constantly transmitting how you feel, your frequency, your light and sound vibration. Everyone feels this, whether they are conscious of it or not. Therefore you and everyone feel or sense everything from everyone. It is the ability to be aware of, discern and interpret the sensate information accurately and consciously that allows a person to experience a full and enjoyable life.

The mental aspect of you is the major influence of your attitudes. Your beliefs created your perceptions of your feelings (both sensate and emotional) which then developed into attitudes.

In other words:

Through your perceptions and beliefs you

made judgments which resulted in attitudes.

Attitudes and Beliefs

Funny thing about attitudes is that they do create beliefs. Attitudes are the emotional components of belief and they can also be the supporter of beliefs which maintains the status of beliefs. An attitude being the emotional component of belief

formation, energetically that is; an attitude is a creative field because it is the emotional field. The emotional field, in this case we are not talking human emotions, we are talking emotional feeling, the sensate feeling, the emotional body that what makes you human.

The human field is an emotional field. It has the components of the mental etc. But the key for the human is their emotional field which is their sensate feeling field not the human emotions such as sadness and grief and happiness. That field is a creative field. It is the womb of your experiences. Whatever you create in that womb will be birth into the experience of your human life.

So if you have a lousy attitude, an unhealthy attitude, whatever we will label it as, you have just birthed an unhealthy experience because, as that attitude sits in your human womb, your emotional field, it turns from a seedling into an actual entity. And after enough time, it is birthed into the experience of a belief and a reality.

Be careful of what you fertilize and give birth to. Your attitudes are key to what you birth in your human experience. And once you have given birth to something then that is in your emotional field as an attitude, we will label it. The more you support that attitude and maintain that way of feeling, the

more you support the belief you just birthed and that experience. But without an attitude that supports a belief, the belief will eventually dry up. When it dries up, it doesn't die; it has the opportunity to be transformed.

Now this is why we have said, "Change your behaviors while you are working on your beliefs because your behaviors are much the way that your attitudes are supported or displayed." And if you change your behaviors, it stops the gross feeding of that belief system or that experience and reality. So you are basically starving it into a place where it needs to transition. So it is much like a starving person can actually kick into an etheric existence without needing food or an alcoholic who goes through a detox. And it is horrible during the detox; but once out of it, they have no more desire or they shift from it if they do not go back into the supporting attitudes.

So this is key to your own creation. To become a creator, you have to be conscious of your thoughts; you have to be conscious of your beliefs. In fact, you actually have to have no belief systems. And then you are to be conscious of you attitudes because your attitudes will just stay in your human womb and create a reality experience that you may or may not be expecting to actually manifest.

Attitudes and the Emotional or Sensate Body

The emotional body is the sensate system of a person, both visible and invisible. The emotional body is more appropriately called the sensate body. It is a sensory system.

Attitudes are the feeling aspect of your thoughts, beliefs and knowings.
Attitudes do not need words to be conveyed.
Attitudes are conveyed feeling through the sensate system of a person.

The sensate body is the energetic, invisible aspect of a person that determines their sensate experience; this includes but is not limited to their emotions. This is the system of sentience, sensuality and sensing. It is through the sensate body that the five physical senses are activated. This system is connected to but not governed by the mental body (the mind). However the mind is often used to attempt to control the sensate body.

Keep in mind that feelings and emotions are two separate yet similar subjects. When we speak of feeling we are referring to your complete sensate experience and emotions: happy, sad, angry, fear etc.

The sensate body is an electromagnetic field that surrounds the physical body. This field senses all the energy/frequencies in your environment. This information is then transmitted to your mind and physical body.

Your mind and physical body interpret and respond to this information based on your beliefs, knowings, soul memory and genetic makeup. This information is technically light and sound vibration. This light and sound vibration also stimulates your DNA/RNA which then activates memories and codes within your DNA/RNA.

The Sensate Experience

So when you are very, very small, we will say up until about three, four years old, depending on the child, everything that you experience in life is a sensate experience. You do not understand words. You do not understand what people mean by the words they are using but you feel what they are projecting with their words and their energy bodies. And you, as a child, respond to those energy bodies not even knowing what you are doing, just sort of on autopilot. Your field gets hit with an energy frequency; your field responds. Internally you decide this feels good; this doesn't feel good.

You make a judgment. You do not have a mental interpretation of that judgment yet; but you make a judgment. Then with that judgment, you move toward and fight, you run away from or you stand and enjoy whichever it might be. But it is a pure response from a sensate experience. It has nothing to do from the words being said. They could be screaming at you in happiness or screaming at you in anger. And all you might be responding to is the scream and the energy of that screaming. Little kids get scared even when they hear really happy loudness. So it does not have to be positive or negative. That does not come until you are able to make a mental judgment on it. All you know is that you like that frequency or you do not. Up until then, you are being programmed with an automatic response to an energy that you feel or sense.

You learn how to respond by mimicking your parent's programs

In the meantime, you are picking up the programs of your parents, and you respond to those frequencies. So now you are going to mimic behavior patterns. And the key here is 'mimic. You are not going to be consciously picking these behavior patterns. You are going to mimic what you have seen mom do, dad, sister, brother, friends, family do. And you are going to select the one that work for you; that make it easiest for you to manage this situation. And all this right now is still sensate. No cognitive or mental understanding of this yet.

Now internally you are having a judgment of whether you like it or it feels good or it does not feel good. But you are not having, "Wow, that is really messed up. I can't believe they are doing that." or "They are really mean." or "They are really hostile." Those judgments are not quite there yet. But you are developing the response pattern to those energies.

Understanding begins
at about six years old.

When you get older, you begin to understand. So around the age of six you start to understand the difference between anger, happiness, and sadness. All those feel different. But now you have a word and you are able to put a word to these simple basic emotions. You still may not like loud happiness even though you now understand that it is happy. You may still be scared or your body may react to the energy to that in an adverse way. But now you are starting to begin to develop a mental judgment of the sensate feelings that you experience.

Realize you have already developed the patterns and a lot of the response mechanisms, likes and dislikes before you could even think this way. Before you could make mental judgments, you were making, what we will call, emotional judgments based upon the comfort-ability you felt with that energy, frequency, behavior or what is being put out in the environment.

Now as you start to develop mentally and you learn words and languaging and you start to understand people's behaviors to a certain degree, you now are putting labels on what you are doing; and beginning to consciously, or still unconsciously, choose behaviors to respond to those energies that you feel from other people. Then you forget all about the sensate feeling and you start to only talk in mental judgment. And you say "Oh I respond to it that way because he was angry. I respond to it that way because she was sad." Now you are speaking from the mental and you are not talking about the sensate or feeling at all.

At this time you learn the feeling automatically. You don't even have words for it so you can't even really discuss it. Adults rarely discuss the feeling or the sensate. At best they will discuss emotions, but it is not the same. Emotions are belief patterns responding to an energy pattern. Now the belief patterns themselves are a sort of energy pattern but we are talking about sensate energy pattern that your body is feeling. And so your body feels a sensate energy pattern; your belief system defines it; and all of the automatic reactions, responses that are in your belief system start to go into action. And if you are lucky, you will be able to consciously choose which ones you are going to use, and which ones are appropriate and not.

But by this time, say around eight to ten years old, this becomes the main focus; it is the mental understanding for most people. Many people still do not have the mental understanding and they are simply emotional, energetic responders. They respond on autopilot without conscious awareness of what they are really feeling or a mental ability to describe and understand what they are feeling. So they are pure responders. Many people grow up in life maintaining that way of behaving. They are simply responders. Something happens; they automatically respond.

People who have gone the mental route tend to judge it; have opinions of it; make a decision and justify why they have done it. But all along, by the time you are an adult, the understanding of your sensate feelings and what you are sensing from the energy of your environment, is almost completely lost. And, at best, often people can only say, "Well, I have a feeling." But they do not understand that it is about the energy. And even when they think that they still have a feeling, they still are using their pattern behaviors and response mechanisms to answer what that energy is that came to them.

So now being an adult who has completely, in most cases, lost your ability to understand the sensate feeling of energy, you have to go backwards. You go in reverse. You have to understand your thoughts, your beliefs, your attitudes, your knowings. You have to then understand where they come from; begin to release them, so to speak; and then you work your way back to looking at them at deeper levels and the root causes of those patterns. And then you go back to the sensate feeling once again.

And now you have come full circle because by the time you have come back to this sensate feeling of energy patterns as an adult, you should be able to acquire the proper languaging system and skills to handle them as well as the ability to make choices on what to do with them and what they really mean to you today. And that is the key, "What does that energy pattern or sensate feeling mean to you today?" Not What did it mean to you at three and you respond to it now as an adult with a mental justification and a judgment; but what does it mean to you actually today? What is the logic of it? What is the reason of it? Does it make sense? Looking at the possible different angles of perception to understand why things might occur and then make a decision on what you are going to do with that feeling.

What does this sensate feeling mean to me today?

Is it logical?

Does it make sense?

Now the mistaken idea is that you have to do anything with that feeling. Technically you don't have to do anything with that feeling. You can just let that feeling go. You can just not respond. You do not have to take that feeling as something that belongs to you.

And here is the misinterpretation. People feel something and they believe that it is theirs without discernment. "I have a feeling. I am feeling angry." Well how do you know it is you? How do you know it is not the five other people in the room that are angry about something and you feel it rather than it's yours? How do you know that it is yours? Did you even take a split second to discern it or did you just respond to the feeling; claimed the feeling as your own; and decide that you had to go into autopilot and do something about the feeling?

People assume that what they are feeling is theirs. And it may not at all be. It may be just that the feeling in the room triggers a feeling you have been harboring within you from a memory of an experience with that energy pattern. For example, somebody yells. When I was a child, I took that feeling as meaning "I was not loved." Now I am an adult, somebody yells. I automatically feel that and respond to it by feeling that I am not loved or wanted when maybe the person was yelling because they were angry with somebody else in the room. Maybe the person was yelling today as an adult because they were frustrated with you that did not complete your job but it had nothing whether they loved you or not.

But you went into the automatic response that I have that feeling, that frequency feels familiar; it means that I am not loved. Then you go into your 'not loved' belief system and you act out in whatever way you do, whether it is sucking up to somebody; whether it is being angry with them or whether it is disappearing and becoming invisible. You go into your auto response pattern because you have felt a frequency that you labeled, judged and go into autopilot every time you feel it. And you did not take the time to discern, "What does it mean to me today?" That is why we use logical, reasonable, and rational as a way to identify what it could mean to you today as an adult or wherever you are today.

But this is really the root of behaviors and beliefs. It is the senate feeling of energy judged and labeled. That is all it is. The root of beliefs is a sensate feeling of an energy that is judged and labeled. And then when you make that instantaneous judgment and it hits the label, you go into the behaviors that are associated with those neural pathways that tell you what to do when you feel that energy. This is the source. And so the reason why we work on beliefs and patterned behaviors is because it backs you out of that automatic response mechanism; it gives you long enough time to make discernments that then you can get into a space of neutrality and not have to respond or claim that feeling as your own; judge it; label and have to respond. It is your freedom. That is why we talk to you about getting to neutral. But this is a process.

It is how you got there and it is how you are getting back. But all of this makes you an energy master, an energy understander. It brings into understanding for you what energy is; what you are. When you are connected to your own Spirit, you do not have to respond to any energy because you are those higher frequencies and those higher frequencies do not need to get involved with the lower frequencies or lower vibrational frequencies. And that is what sets you free.

Become Very Aware of Your Attitudes

Sometimes attitudes are mistakenly confused with volume, passion, intensity, projection or force. Sometimes your attitude could be overlaid on top of your intensity which then would increase the volume of your attitude or the way you feel toward others or feel in your energy field.

If you feel a little snippy, a little cocky, a little down, a little critical, or even if you feel a little too intense, remember you don't have to say a word for it to be felt. Your intensity, criticalness, snippiness or cockiness could just be an attitude it does not have to be expressed. Feeling it is an expression. By feeling something you will naturally express it through your sensate body transmission. Everything you feel is expressed through this way.

There is no way to stop the energetic expression of what you feel!

Become aware of and feel your attitudes. Do your best not to label them as you have learned growing up: "good attitude," "bad attitude," "cocky attitude." It is not about the judgments or labels others reflect to you. It is about the way that your sensate body feels to you and not your emotions.

Your attitude is determined by you and you alone. The way you feel inside determines the attitude you project and what others may feel.
It's all about feeling!

The sensate body is your feeling body; it is your sensing or feeling system.

Emotions are just labels put on sensate feelings, in order to describe and understand those feelings, in order to communicate them to others and make sense of them.

Keep in mind that emotions are created and driven by beliefs and feelings are not the same as emotions, although emotions are felt.

Attitude is a State of Feeling

An attitude at some point was derived from beliefs and perceptions; then it actually comes into a life of its own as it becomes an unconscious way of being without thought. If you have a defensive attitude, an aggressive attitude, a passive attitude these are all feelings you have in your sensate body that you express emotionally. These attitudes are not caused by anything in the present. A present experience does however stimulate the attitude into action.

All attitudes are based on past experiences and judgments.

Attitudes come from long held beliefs, distortions and misperceptions from the past you express sensately, emotionally or through a feeling. Your belief system unconsciously seeks out trigger words, feelings or experiences to respond to in order to support these attitude and beliefs. This typically is a self-protective defense mechanism stemming from a perceived pain, trauma or hurt. The intent is usually, however accurate or inaccurate, to prevent pain from occurring again and to identify potential dangers to avoid. Ultimately most attitudes are fear based.

Focusing on your attitudes is very important in order for you to become conscious. They are often so subtle and discreet that you will only be able to be aware of them if you are conscious of what you are feeling. Attitudes are commonly without thought, they are feeling only, then assumed to be who or what you are, so much so that they are then overlooked. It is common to verbally express an attitude, as the feeling of it comes out along with words. Many people use the statement, "This is who or what I am." as a support to maintain the attitude.

Attitudes are long held beliefs infused with emotion.

You are not your thoughts, beliefs, knowings and attitudes.

These are ways of being, you use to survive and interact with the world. You have created all of them either consciously or unconsciously from a reaction to a perceived event or feeling. Since you have created them, you can change them. Learning and remembering to be the creator you are is available to everyone!

You truly are the Creator of Your Experience.

More about Emotions

Sensate feelings are real. Emotions are not real, even though they are a commonly accepted truth or reality. Emotions are a belief system. In order to communicate and to be understood senate feelings needed a label, many of these labels are what is today called emotions. Unfortunately these labels became truth as the truth and wisdom of the sensate system or emotional body became lost and forgotten.

Again the only reason that people have emotions is because someone labeled the sensate feelings that were commonly experienced. Someone at some point, experienced a feeling long enough to put a name of sadness or happiness on it which then that became the human emotional system. In pure neutrality and wisdom, what is called an emotion is simply a feeling or a sensorial awareness.

Without the judgment of a sensorial awareness, there is no human emotion.

It has been said that, "A human is an emotional being." Human beings, by this definition, are emotional beings. But they are not emotional beings based upon the labels and understandings people have about emotions. Yet for right now, it is what most people can relate to. It is one way for them to understand feeling; it is also one way that they can understand and communicate feelings. It is a standardize level of communication but very inaccurate. A more accurate definition than "A human is an emotional being." is:

A human being is a sensate, sentient,

feeling, sensual being.

Human emotions came from a created belief system that placed a label and judgment on feelings.

Labeling things is a great idea to be able to communicate an experience. However any time you label anything, it is usually turned into a judgment. It therefore has then been limited. It has been contained. It has a box formed around it. Whether it was intended just to communicate or whether it was intended to control, it doesn't make any difference. It still creates a limitation. And because most people are not feeling or conscious of their feeling, they believe in the mental limitation applied to the feeling described and it becomes a paradigm, a belief system and a limitation.

Paradigms, a word unheard of until not that long ago, often times paradigms are seen as positive things. People usually use it in the context of "it's a new paradigm". But let's see it for what it is, "a new box", "a new label," "a new description" that limits the experience.

When you are in absolute feeling, there is absolutely no need to have a paradigm. There is absolutely no need to have a label because it is simply an experience that you appreciate and you move on. That's it, nothing else: an experience appreciated and moved on from.

Patterns

Patterned behaviors are in most cases unconscious responses to external stimuli. Patterned behaviors are learned and assimilated by example, usually by parents or people who are respected or held as authority. Patterned behaviors do not have to be seen in order to be assimilated and believed to be your own. They can be felt intuitively and thereby unknowingly made into an aspect of a person's personality.

Unconscious patterns are hypnotic like states, when you are in them you do not realize you are in them and when you come out of them you wonder what happened. Patterns are set off by triggers. These triggers are 'push buttons,' unconscious reactions to some circumstance; whether it is a look, a feeling, a behavior, a word, a smell, a sound, an action or a deed. Once the trigger occurs patterns are activated. You go into a hypnotic like state and use old behavior patterns to respond to the event. With this type of behavior a person usually believes their interpretation and response is real and accurate.

Trigger: an action or interpretation of an event causing or provoking a perceived need to respond.

Once you have established something as truth then it becomes a patterned behavior. Every applicable event that occurs in your life after that is affected by that perceived truth. People tend to then interpret their life through those patterns, as truthful, real, accurate and factual.

Those interpretations only appear factual based upon your filters or perceptions from and through your patterning and your current beliefs. This is not a truth; nor is it fact.

Patterns may be energetic, mental, emotional, familial, cultural or soul based.

When you realize you have things that bother you (you do not necessarily recognize them as patterns) you usually protect yourself from them. This is often called guarding.

Having your guard up is an attempt to prevent you from being triggered into the states and feelings you do not like and numbs you into the states you do like. Then it is perceived that when you let your guard down bad things will happen and people hurt you.

The truth is, the guard only protects your buttons from being pushed it does not protect you. Because your buttons are protected, and they are not pushed you have the illusion that you were protected. Because of this guard you did not experience any discomfort. The reason you did not feel anything is because your buttons were numbed. In this numb state you were unable to be triggered into an unconscious pattern and feeling that you label as bad, uncomfortable, unpleasant or even miserable. If you were to leave your guard down it would simply mean that your buttons were vulnerable and able to be pushed. Which means that you would unconsciously and automatically react and respond to whatever event triggers your patterned behaviors.

Yet at the same time you do not experience any joy either. So as a coping skill you continue to keep your guard up. The truth is that it is when your buttons are pushed you experience pain and discomfort. Without the buttons you would feel no pain or discomfort. The only way to stop others from hurting you (which they really can't do) is to eliminate your buttons. The only way to feel truly alive is to not be guarded.

Buttons are beliefs and or patterns that trigger you into an unconscious uncontrollable response and reaction.

When you are triggered you then go into the pattern seemingly uncontrollably. You then unconsciously do combat with yourself and your own issues that created the pattern. These issues are usually the beliefs and/or events that originally created the pattern. Next you will unconsciously do combat with yourself internally in order to suppress these memories.

Then as you come out of the pattern you are often angry about having to have gone there, about having to feel the discomfort or pain. As things settle down you also look to see who or what sent you there. The next step is to identify the person, place or thing as the culprit and then attack blame or avoid what or who you believe is the cause of sending you to this unwanted state or feeling.

People usually believe external circumstances are the "cause" for their internal feelings; they then assume that this perception is accurate.

They're not.

You either forget or don't know that if you did not have the pattern or button no one could send you there. We do not look at ourselves to see that it is us who sends us there or even that we created 'there.' It is easier to put the responsibility on someone else. This blame or perception makes you a victim of circumstance.

The pattern of avoiding the fact
that you created your patterns
keeps your life out of control and
keeps you in the state of victimhood.

Remember, when learning to recognize your patterns to be 'an observer not a judge.' Judging yourself for being in a pattern will only keep you trapped in the energy of the pattern. Change can only take place when you are purely observing without the energy of the judgment.

When working with a partner or friend and requesting that they refrain from pushing certain buttons, it is helpful to tell them that this "issue" is your issue but they could assist you with the situation by saying what they need to say in another way. Then give them the exact words to use. This will help to prevent you from going into the pattern so you can work at resolving it. Remember asking for their help is only to buy time until you resolve the problem it is not the solution nor is it their responsibility.

Patterns are unfinished experiences
seeking completion.

There is another type of patterning we would like to mention here.

Energetic and/or Frequency Patterning

Everything in the universe is made up of energy or frequency. This includes thoughts, beliefs, knowings and attitudes. Everything in the universe is an energy or frequency pattern, whether it is understood or not. Your consciousness resonates at a certain energy or frequency pattern based upon the sum total of all of your soul/spirit's experience. Thereby, all of your life experience exists at a particular resonant frequency and due to this you encounter experiences in your human life.

Most people have heard about the law of attraction (this is not an actual law) and we would say to you that the law of attraction is relatively inaccurate yet a good beginning. The law of resonant frequencies (which is also not actually a law) would be more accurate.

The Law of Resonant Frequencies: The frequency and energetic patterning that makes up your consciousness determines your resonant frequency. This personal resonant frequency determines the experiences and potential experiences you will encounter. If you raise your consciousness you raise your vibrational frequency which in turn creates greater potentials in your life.

Ultimately thoughts, beliefs, knowings and attitudes are patterned energetic frequencies. By raising your consciousness you automatically alter these patterns, thereby changing your own thoughts, beliefs, knowing's and attitudes.

Feelings and Patterns

Feelings in a pattern are unconscious
Feelings about the feelings in a pattern are semi-conscious
Feelings about feeling the feelings in a pattern are becoming conscious
Becoming aware or consciousness of the pattern
Clear the patterns to remain conscious

Feelings, if listened to, can be indicators that you are in a pattern.

Five awareness levels of feelings in patterns that lead to consciousness.

1. When feelings in the patterns are unconscious - These are usually connected to experiences before the age of 6, other lifetimes and/or past life memories. These patterns hold connections to your own answers, your feelings and the reason the patterns exist. When you feel things and respond without conscious choice you are governed by your unconscious patterning.

2. Feelings about feeling in patterns are semi-conscious - Feelings about the feelings you have in the pattern: Angry in the pattern, "Life isn't fair." "This sucks. I'm in this anger about not being heard." knowing this allows for the possibility for step three.

3. Your feelings about feelings about the feelings in the patterns, are becoming conscious - Recognizing something is still out of order in your life and you cannot yet make change "I'm upset about being angry and not being heard, my life doesn't feel good, I get that it is part of the pattern." In this stage awareness of, "It doesn't feel right." is the gateway to freedom.

4. **Becoming aware of the patterns -** Awareness of, "I have this feeling and/or pattern and I don't like being in it." You know why and how you are doing what you are doing but cannot yet completely stop it. You begin to get the whole picture. Awareness is the doorway to ending unwanted patterns.

5. **Clearing the patterns -** You consciously start to take apart patterns. Going through window of awareness, reaching down to first level of patterns and begin to cease doing them and begin to restructure them consciously.

> **People blend the levels above in order to unconsciously defend patterns.**
>
> **This is a pattern itself.**

Parenting - Patterned Discordant Energy and Behavior

"The sins of the father are carried on for seven generations" simply means that the patterns or energetic patterning of the parents are carried by each set of children into the following generations. The sins are a metaphor for the discordant patterns or energetic patterned behaviors that are passed on from generation to generation until someone breaks that pattern.

If the parents break the pattern then the children no longer have to carry those patterns. The child will unconsciously feel a relief and will now be able to become who they really are. Otherwise, if you are within that seven generations, you will be living out the patterns of all those previous generations, and not really get to live your own experience unless, **you become aware and decide to consciously break that pattern.**

There are no sins, there are patterns; and if the parent breaks the patterns for the child, the child will automatically intuitively feel that release. If the child is older and they have had those patterns already established and the parent breaks them, they are shown that the possibility exists in this lifetime. They can then pursue the further breaking of the patterns and actually be free of them in this lifetime.

Children believe what adults say. Adults do not realize the power they hold in literally creating life. For what is spoken, seen and felt becomes truth for the child. This then becomes the reality the child is forced to live, until they awaken to themselves. This awakening may or may not occur, so be conscious of what you are creating for your child!

By you, as a parent, breaking your patterned behaviors you release your children from those patterns no matter what age they are. By providing them with the experience energetically or by their witnessing you change, you teach them they can change those patterns. This creates the potential and the opportunity for them to be free. If you physically die before doing that in this lifetime, it is their journey alone without relief. They will unconsciously carry on those patterns into the next generation and so on and so on and so on.

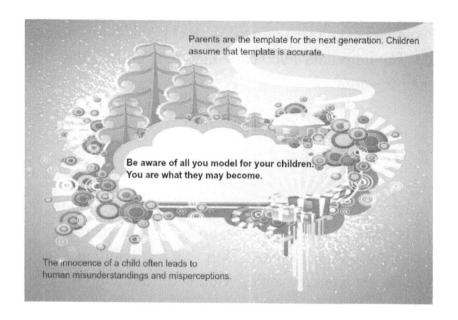

Parents are the template for the next generation. Children assume that template is accurate.

Be aware of all you model for your children. You are what they may become.

The innocence of a child often leads to human misunderstandings and misperceptions.

The sooner you break your patterns, the younger your children are the greater opportunity for a lifetime of freedom you create for your child. As you break the pattern, teach your child consciously. Verbally communicate what the pattern was, why it was there, how you got it, how you misperceived it, how you passed it to them. Then tell them how they got it, how they misperceive it, how they integrate it into their life. This will expedite their freedom. Because not only have you broken the pattern or eliminated the "sin", you have given them all the keys necessary to open any doorway they want into the potentials of their life.

Breaking your patterns is a magnificent gift to your child and to you. Breaking the pattern and giving the information you give to your child is a chest of gold. In fact it has more value than gold. The inheritance you pass on to your child is the gift of their freedom.

Mom & Dad Patterns

On the other hand, when you compare yourself or you look at mom's patterns or dad's patterns, do not look at them as saying, "They gave them to me." Don't look at blaming them. You do not want to blame. What you want to do is look at them and compare what you do to what they did in the sense of "How did it work for them? How did they do it? "Wow, I can understand me now by looking at their patterns." Their patterns simply become a frame of reference.

Too many people make the parents' patterns an excuse or a frame of blame. You should use the parents' patterns as a frame of reference not a frame of blame. People tend to fall into looking at their parents' patterns as they are either blaming them or that, "It is the reason I have this problem."

You have to remember that you came into this life to learn something or to complete something. Therefore your patterns came from your parents who generously, in a funny way, donated all of their messed-up patterns to you so that you could learn what you came here to learn not to deliberately screw you up. But in the human sense, you got screwed up from them. So this is why you need to look at the patterns differently and your parents in a different frame of references.

It is okay to look at them just as a frame of reference. (Learn more about parenting, how you were parented and breaking patterns on the book, Change Your Mind, Not Your Child.)

Behaviors

Behaviors are only the representative of beliefs and patterns. They have no foundation without the belief or a pattern and patterns are run by beliefs.

Behaviors are only the external manifestation of presenting or expressing the belief to the world. They are temporary, can be altered very easily. They can be used to hide true feelings and intents or used to con others. This works because people tend to look at behaviors and assume them to be real while very seldom "feeling" what is really going on. People have been taught to disbelieve their feelings or intuition and to trust words and behaviors instead.

It is why people can be duped, because they are not looking past the behaviors. As they are looking at other's behavior they are seeking to get a need met. The need (based on their belief) to be a victim, abused, noticed, acknowledged, etc. The behavior allows them to get what they perceived they need. So they enter an unwritten agreement to not look past the behaviors in order to get their needs met and then blame the other person for being evil or deceptive as a way to avoid looking at their own participation in the event.

Trust your Intuition
but hone your interpretation skills.

Even though behaviors may be based on the original, unconscious beliefs, they can become conscious actions you use in your human life. Once you no longer believe your beliefs, you can use the behaviors that you learned while your beliefs turn to awarenesses as tools to integrate with the world and interface with other human beings.

The choice is yours. You can remain in these patterned beliefs that you have assumed are true, operating your life unconsciously or you can seek truth. Then consciously choose the behaviors you wish to use while interfacing with the world and creating the life you want.

Patterns and beliefs once released

become human skills!

Release of Patterns

There is much talk about ways to have what you want. If these ways work for you use them. However what we have found is that in order to really have what you want it is necessary to clear your unwanted patterns. You should however be aware of the fact the most patterns operate unconsciously. Therefore you must become conscious of them. This means you may need assistance in doing so and you must diligently exercise your self-awareness

skills. One way to do this is to be aware of your every thought and correlate your thought patterns with the way you feel. Keeping a journal of your thought is helpful too.

Most people have made an identity of who they believe they are, the characteristics they are supposed to embody, the behaviors they are supposed to have. To dismantle that is quite scary. In fact it can be devastating.

The purpose of shifting your beliefs is not to dismantle this; it is to expand you to see more. So if you could understand or the ego personality could understand that as the beliefs get dismantled you don't lose the skills you've gained. But what you do loose is the identity of who you thought you were. And in that, it appears as if you are losing a grip, so to speak. But the truth is that your grip is actually expanding to something greater so that you can see and be more rather than be the less that you thought you were.

So as the beliefs are dismantled, it makes space for awareness which then makes space for consciousness. And in consciousness, you still retain all of the wisdom and the skills that you have gained through experience. But the 'little I' or the ego personality tends to not really see that; so it tends to hold on. And as it holds on in a contracting type of way, it holds onto the fabric, the energetic fabric that has knitted the personality. And so as it holds on to that, any expansion feels like tearing or hurting or dangerous.

But if it could just breathe and stretch, it could see that it could be bigger and taller or more expansive and still be the same yet be different. And that is the irony there, that expanding to be more and different yet being the same within that expansiveness. Very abstract, it is very difficult for the ego personality to grab and grasp.

A brief personal story: For me one of the oldest and dearest patterns to let go of was what I call the warrior pattern. I was very attached to it and was even proud of owning it. It was a source of perceived strength, power and kept me safe (so I thought). Although, in a way it did

keep me safe on a human level by keeping foes or danger at bay and often intimidating adversaries and with it I would follow through where others would only talk.

The hardest part of letting it go was that it was like a dear friend that served me loyally at all times without question. In many ways it was something I did not want to let go of because of its devoted service to my human self and the belief that without it life might be dangerous and scary. I was taking a risk letting it go, it was like standing naked in front of the world with no defense. I had to truly trust my own spirit as I have never trusted before.

It has been my experience that it is like this for all of us as we let go of our most trusted patterns. The patterns that have helped us navigate the world; the ones we believe protect us are the most difficult to change. To be exposed without them can be terrifying; in fact so much so it may seem impossible for some people to let them go. The fear may be so great that an individual may not even be able to bring awareness of the pattern to their consciousness. They often see it as part of who they are not as a separate pattern. The essence of the release is the same, even if the pattern is different, for any and all core patterns.

1. Become conscious of the pattern
2. Identify it
3. Change your ways of thinking and your behaviors
4. Find the source of its beginning
5. Identify the need it fulfills
6. Visualize the need fulfilled without it
7. Though a visualization change the originating experience

Clearing your patterns is a process that begins with taking responsibility for your life, your choices, your behaviors. It is what we work on in the Human Mastery Course (see our website for more information, www.livingconcepts1.com .)

Taking responsibility for yourself and the changes you want is the only way to have the life you want.

10 Warning Signals of Being in an Unconscious Pattern

1. When what you're experiencing feels familiar.

2. Looking to the outside for answers.

3. Seeing or believing that your 'I AM' presence is separate from you.

4. Gathering information from others or outside of yourself.

5. You are not self-reflecting and the information you're gathering does not come from internal reflection.

6. Being focused on circumstances and minute details.

7. All that you're experiencing is going on inside your head.

you have done enough of your own work. When you have done enough of your own work, the belief pattern or belief system has been altered. And after it has been altered, sometimes you still have habit patterns which could appear as thoughts. So we will say they are strayed neural pathways that are running old thoughts that don't even exist in the root system any more or in the belief system anymore.

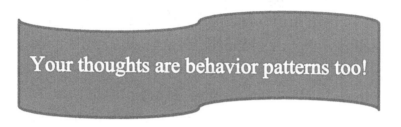

Your thoughts are behavior patterns too!

And then you act out based upon those thoughts. Why? Because you are not conscious; because you are assuming they are still real; because you are assuming they are still truths. So now you act out on them and you say, "Oh I am still acting out." Well no, you are acting out because you are not conscious. What's consciousness going to do? Consciousness is going to give you the ability to discern whether it is really a belief system or it is simply a thought process that is still a random habit that you haven't become conscious of.

It is sort of like when you are with other people and you feel depressed, let's say as an example, and you know that you are not depressed but you feel really depressed and you go, "Wow, I am depressed." That would be an automatic habit; a lack of consciousness. That would be not discerning if you were truly depressed or there was depressive energy in the room that you were in. And then determining whether you want to be affected by it or not. That is what consciousness will do for you. That will set you free. Remember consciousness is the cure to everything.

And we are not talking conscious awareness like, "Oh I am aware of the wall in front of me" or "I am aware of driving." We are talking about expanded consciousness, the connection between your human ego personality and your I AM Presence or your Spirit, that consciousness. And from that connected consciousness, you are able to discern which is you; which is not you; which is a habit pattern; which is still a belief system; which is still some process in your energy body memory or soul memory that hasn't been, we will say, altered yet.

So now it is time for you to kind of step up the pace and say "Okay, I have to check now. I won't assume that every feeling that I am having is real. I will not assume that every feeling I am having is true or that every feeling or thought that I am having is really mine." You need to begin to discern the differences.

Not every feeling you have
is real or even yours!

Here is the place where discernment becomes a skill. Before, it was a tool. So we were teaching it as a tool so you could get to the place where it became a skill. Once it becomes a skill, the ability to sort out these random habit patterns and then make conscious choices becomes easier. Then you get to actually choose your experience.

Let's talk about body memory; body memory simply meaning not that the body has a mind of its own, but that it has a sensate remembrance of experiences. And the sensate remembrance is about a certain frequency that occurs. So when your body and we are not talking just your physical body now we are talking your energy bodies, all of them. When your energy bodies have had an experience, they store the memory. It's passed on to your physical body. Your body holds that memory in its cells as well.

And so when you are in it, or when you are not in it, and you are moving around the world, so to speak, and your body encounters a certain frequency or experience or is put into a position, it sensately feels what going on; associates that with the other experiences that are stored; and then the body reacts. So this is where the body would shake even though in your mind you know it doesn't make any sense.

We will also say that it is stored in the subconscious because again without a head your body wouldn't be reacting. So the subconscious is kind of the recorder of that memory but it is also may be stored in the cells of the body or in the frequency of your energy body patterning. And once you change the energy body patterning that is how you alter that as well.

In most cases you can alter it through altering your belief systems. But sometimes the body has had an experience that has nothing to do with this time. And that program is in your soul memory which is still stored in what is called your energy bodies. And your body responds to certain frequencies, settings or experiences even though your mind does not agree or knows that it doesn't make any sense.

> Talk to your body,
> "This is not your truth.
> This is not your experience now."

And this is the place where you talk to your body. Now you are not simply talking to your physical body. You are talking to your energy bodies; and your body meaning, we will say, all of you. You're talking to your body as a plural. And you are telling it, "This is not your truth. This is not your experience. This is not the present. This is not the way it is this day and time. This was an experience from which you can extract the wisdom, but you do not need it to protect yourself, fear or respond to these types of frequencies anymore, ever again. It is not required."

And so it is a way that we would say that you talk to your body but it is more than talking to your body. And that will assist in that habit patterns also because this would be an unconscious habit pattern. The energy body responds to a frequency, to a setting, to an encounter. And you then interpret it and it gets distorted. So we say to you that talking to the body; looking and discerning for random patterns versus beliefs or still perceived truths; and identifying which it is. Once it becomes understood by you and your bodies, then it will stop.

And much of this stuff that you have carried through is not from this place. So many times it won't make logical sense especially the ones that randomly, seemingly randomly, continue. So this is really your ability to be a creator and direct your body, your experience and your own process as opposed to be subject to automatic responses that are simply random habit patterns that hold no basis in truth or reality any longer.

Consciousness Cures Everything.

✝ Freedom from Limitation

Every process that you have ever seen or ever will see is just a step heading to the freedom from limitation. No process is permanent, no process is the ultimate. All processes are simply the step to the next step. And for the final step, well... there is no step. There is just endless experience of anything and everything.

There is only ultimate creatorship, where you are in tune with your divinity, with your divine nature; and you are beyond all levels of consciousness that require steps, stages or processes. This is what we will label as freedom for now.

When you are free of your thoughts, beliefs, knowings and attitudes you will experience pure awareness; from here you can create limitlessly and experience with a new-found joy.

Creating a New Paradigm

The best place to start is with a new understanding of the world and of you. In this new paradigm, you are not a victim or powerless over your life. You have the ability to make change because everything you do, have ever done and believe is a product of your own creation. This may sound contrary to everything you've learned.

Making Change - The key to understanding this new paradigm is to know that you believe your beliefs are true, when really they are not. Most of the time they are illogical and emotionally based, they are not even based on reality. But they have become the foundation for your belief systems, behaviors and patterns. Therefore they have become the foundation of your life. In the end, these beliefs affect all areas of your life: work, relationships, parenting, even your health.

When you begin to see that your beliefs are the cause of many of your problems in life, you can begin to clear and change them. The best way to make lasting change in your life is to go back to the beginning of your life. The idea is to trace back the root of these beliefs and the patterns they are causing to clear them. The book, *The 55 Concepts, A Guide to Conscious Living* is a tool to help you uncover these subconscious patterns and beliefs.

From The 55 Concepts: *"Problems only come from our perceptions and the meaning we put to our perceptions. All answers we need are within because we can spiritually access the answers."*

Conclusions

Beliefs, thoughts, and knowings are frequencies you carry with you through all your life experiences. Some assume they are our destiny; and that things will never change.

Things only change as you change.

You must always question everything. The best things to question are the things you have never questioned. Question to find the source. The only time people are not willing to question something is when they are hiding or fear something. Be curious, inquisitive, and open like a child who is pure in nature.

Pay attention to evidence. Avoid skipping past what you see just because you have already concluded or believed something. Remember that you support your beliefs by the way you interpret and respond to events.

Your story will support your beliefs
AND
your beliefs create your reality!

Exercises

- What childhood beliefs do you live today and still perceive?
  If these beliefs are in one part of your life they are in others to a greater or lesser degree, you must deal with them in all aspects of your life (i.e. relationships, work, money, health, etc). When you see something and know it to be true, recognize and know it is one of your beliefs and then ask yourself why you believe it.

- What do you really believe? List as many beliefs as you can. Stretch to find those you aren't even aware you have.

- What level of beliefs do my beliefs come from?

- What pattern keeps repeating in my life that is not working?
  What beliefs are behind it?

- Read this book several times. You will receive new perspectives and understandings when you do.

This is an ongoing exercise, the more you do it the more you realize! To learn about changing beliefs see the book, *The Seven Steps to Freedom*.

Read *As a Man Thinketh* by James Allen, available free on the internet.

Read and apply daily the concepts from *The 55 Concepts, A Guide to Conscious Living*. Application of the Concepts alone can change your life.

To Infinity and Beyond...

In this section you will find material that will stretch your thinking and beliefs beyond all that has been written before.
Take in as much or as little as works for you.

Core Patterns, Beliefs and Identities

People are looking for "the" core pattern as if there is one or as if there is a shortcut. There is no shortcut! There is no one core pattern or belief. There is one common belief and pattern and that is: "I am separate from God/Source".

All the other "core" things that people are talking about as core patterns or beliefs are simply part of a giant group of beliefs which are so enmeshed with the individual' identity and persona, that they cannot be seen or recognized.

You will have to read this next sentence several times and very carefully as it is a bit of a riddle: Because you *believe* you are, who you *believe* you are, you cannot see *the beliefs that make up who you believe you are.*

As the peripheral ones that are evident and circumstantial come up in your life you can start to see. "Oh yeah, I believe that people shouldn't litter." or I believe that you should recycle." or "I believe that relationships don't last." or whatever it might be, those are the obvious easy ones.

It will be more difficult to see the beliefs that you believe you are because you still believe you are who you thought and have been told you are. Until you conceive of or stop believing that you are who you thought you were, the 'little you', the 'you' with the name Frank, Jack or Mary etc., you are not going to realize or see the patterns that make up who you believe you are. *You are a grand magnificent being far more capable and gifted than you currently believe you are.*

You have to really start to get you are not the named identity you have been given. And you are not all of the associated characteristics that go along with the named identity you have been given such as Mary or Nancy or Jack or Joe. You are not that identity. And until you

can really be able to conceive that you are not that, getting to your 'core' patterns is virtually impossible.

Imagine actually getting to the belief that things are solid. Well, that would pretty much eliminate a lot of identities because then you would have to realize your body isn't really solid; and you actually have to have the experience of, or cellular experience of your body rather than the physical matter of your body; and you wouldn't be limited by walls or water or space or time. That's pretty huge because now I wouldn't need a car; I wouldn't need a plane; I wouldn't need a house. I could create all these things and go into them; but I don't need them the way I do when I experience those as real beliefs that exists.

Core beliefs are those beliefs which are so enmeshed with your identity that you can't see them.

Getting to your core patterns is pretty complex. Without them you may not be able to function very well, at least until you rediscover how to integrate your true self with your human skills. This is why people often can't actually get to core beliefs.

Yes, it is somewhat easy to reach beliefs like, "I am not good enough." I am not lovable." or "I am unworthy." Those are pretty big beliefs and they are core beliefs for the ego personality in the way it functions. But they aren't core beliefs of an identity.

In most cases it is optimal to go through a gradual undoing of beliefs. This makes it easier for the ego personality to adjust. Fast 'deprogramming' is often too traumatic for the ego personality to deal with and remain functionally intact.

Some core beliefs of the identity are:
- you actually have and are a solid physical form
- you can't walk through walls
- you will sink if you walk on water

These are core beliefs of being human, not ego personality core beliefs. So we would then need to differentiate between ego personality beliefs, ego personality core beliefs and human being core identity beliefs.

Some of those human core identity beliefs are aging, illness, death etc. Imagine if you actually deleted the core human identity beliefs of aging, illness and death. Wow, that would freak a lot of people out! It would also be pretty weird to accept because, who could believe that you could actually not believe that and live as long as you wanted? That would be quite challenging because that is a major identity shift.

- *Who are you then?*

- *Who are you if you do not die, do not get ill and do not age?*

- *Can you imagine living in absolute health with everything you could ever need?*

- *Who are you if you have 'magical powers' that can only be used for love and creation?*

- *Who are you if you are limitless?*

- *Can you handle that kind of freedom???*

You may think this all sounds crazy, but so was flying 200 years ago!

To eliminate just the three beliefs about aging, illness and death would incredibly change the entire experience of the planet. You could actually live here as long as you wanted to live and enjoy yourself without complications. You would still have to learn to interact with other human beings who may or may not be aware of these truths. So, there are the human skills again, ever so important. Even if you were free from death, aging, and illness, you would still need the human skills to interact here to enjoy the richness of being human.

People often look for the one answer that will change everything. We would say to you the only answer is the knowing that you are a Divine Being and you are not separate from Source; you are Source. That absolute knowing changes everything. However, if that

occurred too fast it would quite literally decimate the ego personality structure, at least at this time in evolution. So, gradual change is optimal at this time.

Core Patterns, Beliefs, Identity and Dismantling Beliefs

Most people have an identity of who they believe they are. This is a belief system. The characteristics they are supposed to be, the behaviors they are supposed to have. If you were to dismantle this identity it would typically be quite scary. In fact it can be devastating if done too fast or impatiently. But the optimal way to change, is to change your beliefs- not dismantle your identity.

The purpose of shifting your beliefs is not to dismantle the identity. It is to remodel it, to expand your awareness to see and experience more. So if your ego personality could understand that as the beliefs get dismantled you don't lose the skills you've gained or the things you like. But what you do lose is the identity of who you thought you were supposed to be. In that, it appears as if you are losing a grip, so to speak. But the truth is that your grip is actually expanding onto something greater. You can see and be more rather than be the limited person you thought you were.

So as the beliefs are dismantled, it makes space for awareness which then makes space for consciousness. In consciousness, you still retain all of the wisdom and the skills that you have gained through experience. But the 'little I' or the ego personality tends to not really see that; so it tends to hold on. As it holds on in a contracting type of way, it holds onto the fabric; the energetic fabric that has knitted the personality. As it holds on to that, any expansion feels like tearing, hurting or dangerous. This holding on is fear. This fear creates anxiety and tension in the body while often creating panic in the mind. This will often bring up feelings like: fear of death, impending doom, fear of the unknown, etc.

There is no such thing as fear of the unknown! Think about it, if it is unknown how can you fear it? Fear of the unknown is a projection of something you are afraid to see or feel, either consciously or unconsciously, onto a completely new potential you have yet experienced.

But if the ego personality could just breathe and stretch, it could see and realize that it could be bigger, grander or more expansive while being the same yet being different. That is the irony here, expanding to become more and different yet remaining the same within that expansiveness. Very abstract, eh?

This is very difficult for the ego personality to grab and grasp. This is where being heart centered comes in. This heart is not emotional: it is not what human love is portrayed to be. The heart we speak of is something greater. Something Christ and the ancient masters spoke of.

- *The heart is where your spirit/soul resides.*
- *The heart is the center of you, your universe.*
- *The heart is the source.*
- *The source of you.*
- *The heart is the seat of wisdom and intuition.*

Become the heart and all your inner wisdom is remembered!

Frequency Mastery - Energetic Patterns, Beliefs, Thoughts and Frequency

You have learned about beliefs and thoughts because it was a way for us to lead you back to understanding your frequency. Beliefs are the clothing for your frequencies; just like your skin is the housing for your spirit.

It is time for you to understand about frequency itself and to have dominion over your frequency. Part of that still includes getting rid of your old belief systems, your old emotions and your attachments. Yes, all that is still included. But you need to get closer to the source here. So it is very important that you pay attention to your thoughts and your beliefs on a regular basis. It is very important for you to pay attention to those people who are mirroring you back to you. And then have the ability to discern if it is a mirror or an observation. In most cases they are mirrors of some kind.

A frequency master will be able to observe what others are doing without it being a mirror. You will have momentary glimpses of that, but as a whole it is best if you assume you are not there yet. As a frequency master, you can experience all kinds of different frequencies without being affected by them. But it is all too easy for people to assume they are a master and assume that the frequencies they are experiencing belong solely to others. This is a precarious part of the process. Never assume you are something you are not. If you were a master now you would not be reading this information.

For right now 'Assume nothing.' Just assume that everything you are experiencing is still to some degree a mirror of you. Temporarily use this assumption as a personal safety mechanism while you go through the narrow strait of the ego-personality. Otherwise you will lose yourself saying "Oh, that is not me; that's them. I am just observing them."

This goes back to the Concept,

"Be an observer not a judge."

This is another level of that understanding. (reading *The 55 Concepts, A Guide to Conscious Living will explain in greater detail*)

Frequencies, energetic fields, energy bodies are, in essence, electromagnetic fields that surround or make up the physical body.

Your thoughts are resonant frequencies. Whatever thoughts you have, have a particular frequency. Yes, your thoughts stem from beliefs and your thoughts, beliefs, knowings and attitudes combined equals your frequency. Your current frequency patterning is who you are as a creator at any given moment; and this is the sum total frequency of you. This frequency patterning determines how you experience the world and determines what inner talents you can manifest.

Your beliefs are the embodiment of those frequencies. And your thoughts are the creations and manifestations of those frequencies that then turn them into your experience. So by being aware of all those things, it gives you the ability to direct your life and create consciously and become a conscious creator as opposed to an unconscious victim of your own creations.

You walk around in thoughts that you don't even pay attention to. They are not only a reflection of a belief system you have; but they are also a manifesting frequency. As you continue those thoughts, it strengthens and resonates the frequency of your energy field to the frequency or level of consciousness that you are focused on or that unconsciously operate, which then provides a resonant frequency in your body and/or energy bodies that then energetically attracts events and experiences of an equivalent nature.

Then you experience circumstantial events in your human world or encounters with other people and other things, that are actually result of the frequency of the thoughts and beliefs mirroring your sum total energetic frequency.

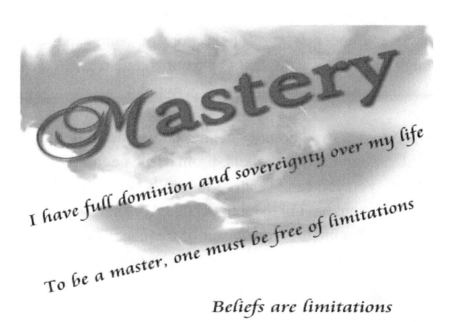

Mastery

I have full dominion and sovereignty over my life

To be a master, one must be free of limitations

Beliefs are limitations

Frequency is the source of everything. Beliefs give you the ability to manifest that frequency. thoughts create the manifestation of that frequency, which   in turn shows up in your physical experience in varied experiences or encounters from emotional, physical, mental or circumstantial. So by changing your sum total frequency, you get to change your experience. Being conscious of your thoughts and your beliefs allows you to be able to be a conscious creator.

At the beginning of this information we covered, thoughts, beliefs, knowings, attitudes, family patterns as a way to bring you to this understanding about frequencies. Now you are on the edge of a new and greater awareness, where you can begin to learn something different. Understand that beliefs are simply a display of your frequencies; that beliefs are not really the source, frequencies are at the core of your experience. Through the beliefs, you can alter your frequencies. At least until you get to the neutral point or zero point.

When you are at zero point or neutral point, you are at no thought, no mind and no beliefs. From a true neutral point frequency, you you can use all of the skills you have acquired without having to be the skills. At neutral point you create from intent. As a master of frequency you may use any frequency to design rather than be in the frequency to be in order to use it.

Beliefs are the intangible embodiment of energetic patterning. The energetic patterning is so non-physical, intangible that it can't even be described at this point except through maybe quantum physics. Beliefs up until to now were virtually unspoken of and almost never seen as a source of creating. Typically all that was perceived by most people were behaviors or the words being used.

But humanity is at the point where they do understand beliefs; that they exist and how they actually affect and create experience. It is becoming very acceptable these days. Behavior modification is now becoming obsolete. What is really needed to be studied and developed is belief modification. There should be a whole new psychological field of belief modification.

Just as behaviors are the embodiment of the belief, beliefs are the embodiment of energetic patterning.

When a person really knows and understands energenetics, they will be able to alter the energetic patterning, thereby automatically changing the belief system, thereby automatically changing the behaviors and thereby automatically changing the outcomes.

Technically speaking, changing beliefs or the belief work that is available today is a way of altering the energetic belief system and changing the energy patterns. As humanity evolves they will discover new ways of change that will make even these 'modern' methods look antiquated. Belief Modification will eventually replace traditional therapy!

Frequency Mastery - Mastering Your Patterned Behaviors

Changing beliefs and altering the patterns that you currently have, is freeing you from the patterns not eliminating the patterns. The patterns that you have are like skills, if used properly. That skill set is important to being human; hence, you are Mastering the Art of Being Human.

You have to have skill sets in order to interface with life on earth and those skill sets are actually patterned frequencies. The major problem now is that most people believe they are those frequencies. When you believe you are those patterns and you base your life on what the patterns tell you you're supposed to do and be, you are sort of imprisoned or entrapped by those patterns and not using them as tools.

Patterns as skill sets - What you may want to be doing is releasing yourself from your patterns so that you can use them as skill sets, like tools. For example: if is appropriate to behave a certain way at a restaurant that is what you can do or if you need to behave a certain way at a meeting, you can do so. If you need to behave a certain way in your job, you can do so because you have those patterned skill sets to use.

Detachment - As you feel the separation from your patterns, at first it's stunning, it's mystifying, it kind of leaves you in "What do I do?" "Who am I?" Sometimes you get into judgment of the patterns, saying how bad they were and how they imprisoned you. You may even go into, "I am never going to use those again!" or "They were wrong." If you go into judgment of them, you have to go through the process of loving them, knowing that you created them, that they have a use, that you are the skill master, you are not the skill. You cannot become whole if you reject any aspect of yourself.

As the skill master, you can use any pattern that you want to use based upon any given day and situation you are in to your benefit. You use those skills to create and manifest the world you want to have, not the one that you are subject to, you were unconscious of or believed you were. You are now able to make conscious creative choices using the skills you have learned.

Detaching from your patterns creates a new sum total frequency which enables you to more consciously create!

Clarity - To clarify: having patterns is not bad or wrong. They are not the bad guys; they are not something to war against.

127

They are something that you misunderstood, misinterpreted and began to believe in as if they were false gods. They are only false gods that corrupted your world and your life because you made the choice to be unconscious.

In order to become a conscious creator being, you have to be free from that enslaved belief system that you are these patterned behaviors or beliefs. Then you can use those beliefs and patterns as skill sets to do whatever you want on planet earth.

The reason it is optimal to get rid of patterned behaviors is because you believed yourself to be them. You had to free your consciousness, from the limiting belief of being those patterns.

When you get to the next level you can realize that all those patterned behaviors that you judged as good or bad, lousy or wonderful were all just judgments that kept you limited. You then can select the sets of skills or patterns that work to create your world.

In the beginning, one might look at these patterns as things you need to be free from because that is the start. It is where you consciousness is at that time. As you grow and expand you realize that you have become free from those patterns.

Beyond Beliefs

What people don't understand is that beliefs and the belief work is simply another stage. It is not the end all, be all. Beyond beliefs is **You.** Now if you don't act on what you have uncreated or created, then they will go into auto-pilot; and they will regrow whatever way they are going to regrow. So there is too much emphasis at this point; but it is a stage for people to learn about beliefs, belief systems. They are beyond thoughts. They are beyond behaviors. Now you have to understand there is something beyond beliefs. And that is **You**.

And until you take action and create deliberately and consciously, you will just have an auto-pilot of some form of those beliefs reformed simply out of you not taking care of it yourself. You still don't get how you are creators and people in generally don't. And they may not for a long time.

But you have to understand that you are literally creators. And even though you eliminate old beliefs or neutralize the energy of them for now, what are you going to operate on if you don't do anything? If you make no decision on what you are going to do and direct yourself then what are you going to do? You are going to sit there like a lump or you are just going to unconsciously allow some belief system to form so you have something to operate with; and usually it will be version of the old beliefs you were neutralizing. So don't get lost in that,

"Beliefs are the end of everything. They are the answer to everything." No, it is just another stage.

You are the Creator. What will you create?

Beliefs are not Necessary, Understanding Them Is - Beliefs exist and are the standard operating system for this world and others; but they are neither necessary nor required to operate. However an understanding of the belief systems of each dimension you are in is required in order to navigate it comfortably. But as you reach the understanding of beliefs in this world, you will eventually get to the place of knowing that there is something beyond belief. And that is the knowing. Then beliefs will become obsolete. Beliefs are polarized. Knowing is unity.

Beyond Beliefs is Consciousness - Beyond beliefs is your consciousness, pure absolute consciousness. The consciousness of your Spirit is beyond beliefs. So when someone says to you, "Yes, it is beyond belief." That is true. It is beyond belief this type of consciousness. You don't have to believe in it. You don't have to have any formation of structured thought. There is simply an awareness and a knowingness about all things that need to be known.

Beyond Beliefs – Knowingness - So being in this new creatorship is not about a belief. You do not have to believe in it. And there is a place beyond belief. And so that phrase is really true, "Beyond belief." Well, that is the next stage we are heading to - is an existence beyond believing. Beyond belief is the knowingness; is just the awareness of All. This is different than the knowingness we talked about earlier which was about beliefs.

And so to get to the creatorship or be the creator that you are, there is no need to believe anything. In fact beliefs would be limiting. So to believe in being a creator would limit your creatorship. Without beliefs you could just be all things. Then all things would be possible and no beliefs would be required. So being a true creator is actually a place beyond belief, beyond believing. All beliefs are limiting no matter how positive they may appear.

Knowing is limitless. There is no limitation to knowing. And so to believe that you have to believe that you are a creator limits you. It means that you are not. So if you were struggling to believe in who you are or believe that you have memory beyond this consciousness, then you are struggling for a new limitation. There is truly nothing to believe in. There is only the knowingness of the All. And when you tap into that, there is limitlessness and you are free from all limitations.

But this transpires through many levels of existence not just the human existence. Because even at other levels, or dimensions, there are limits to their consciousness based upon the dimensional awareness they are in unless they are connected to the All and then just bring that into the dimensional awareness they are existing in currently. Then they have access to the All and are unlimited in any dimensional travel or experience they so choose.

So you could say this, if you are going up in consciousness, each level that you are going up in frequency brings you to a next level of limitation ever expanding. But if you have reached the All, then there is no limit and you may descend into each level of existence remaining connected to the All and never being limited yet appearing limited in each dimension you are existing in.

There is no limit to knowingness.

Freedom from Limitation
is
Your Divine Birthright

The Journey

The first step of the journey is to become aware of your patterns.

The second step of the journey is to get free of your patterns.

The third and most important step of the journey would be to not judge your patterned behaviors.

The fourth step would be to decide what you want to create in your life.

The fifth step is to decide what tools of your patterned behavior skill sets are you going to use to create what you want to create.

The sixth step is to create.

The seventh step is to sit back and enjoy what you have created.

Enjoy the journey!

Section II

Ego Personality, Conscious & Unconscious

Overview

In this section we will touch on the ego, the personality, conscious awareness, different types of truth and the basics of how the conscious and unconscious minds work, as well as how they interact. You will get the basics on how to identify, understand them and what it means to integrate them with your spirit in order to become all you can be.

You must keep in mind that the conscious and unconscious operate on thoughts, beliefs, knowings, attitudes and soul memory.

Reminder:

Thoughts - thinking, ideas, interpretation of perceptions, mental activity, judgments or opinions.

Beliefs - assumed truths, based upon personal conscious and unconscious awareness, as well as the collective conscious and unconscious assumed truths of humanity.

Knowings - the unquestioned assumed truths that are related to the collective unconscious of humanity and the unconscious assumed truths based upon the soul memories.

Soul Memory- the memories of all the experiences an individual's soul has ever had since it left Source/God.

Thoughts, beliefs, knowing and soul memory at their core are simply patterned frequencies. Each person's set of patterned frequencies is different and unique unto each person's own experiences and soul memories.

Core Belief for All Human Beings

We would suggest that there is actually only one core belief that underlies all other beliefs. This belief we will call the "human identity belief". This belief is the source of all human identities. The Human Identity Belief:

I am separate

Along with this belief is one other belief that we believe is equally important yet makes the same statement:

I am separate from God/Source

These beliefs in truth are actually commands that manifest and create the illusion of separateness. At one time this was the only way to manifest as a human being and be able to have separate perceptions and experiences that were unique to your own soul or spirit. This was a departure from the original creation where all souls knew they were part of Source.

This belief system sets the foundation for each individual to have the need to feel special, unique or better than, as well as create the perception that some people are less than, not good enough, not special, etc. The second, most important belief for human beings:

I believe what I believe and perceive it to be true

This belief states that you are believing what you perceive and believe it to be the truth and the way it is without question. Without this belief the ego could not exist nor could your personality or the perception of who you think you are remain intact.

The first and core belief "I am separate" is the belief that you accepted as truth when you left the knowing of the oneness of Source. It is with this belief that you have the opportunity to have the human experience.

The second "I believe what I believe/perceive to be true" is the reason life is the way it is for you. You create and experience your life through this belief. It is what the ancients meant by "Life is an illusion." The illusion is and that you believe what you think you see and assume it to be true and therefore experience what you think you see as real.

The Ego

All human beings have an ego also known as the basic self, the lower self and many other names. In this culture the ego will probably be the best known and easiest understood.

Sometimes when people mention the ego you may hear: "He is so full of himself." or "She is so egotistical." This is a form of pride not the ego, although the ego uses pride to feel good about itself; as well is to compensate for feeling bad about itself.

The ego's nature is to withdraw or defend against that which it perceives threatens its identity or existence. Some examples of what the ego sees as threats are: love, intimacy, change or anything that implies or creates unity. The ego perceives unity as the elimination of self, which is a false understanding. Unity is the act of uniting while experiencing this unity through an individuated consciousness.

The ego is the beliefs and perceptions of an individual that tell them who they think they are or who they are supposed to be. In essence the ego is an identity. It is a temporary identity because it only lasts as long as you are the human being you believe you are. After death this type of ego ceases to exist.

What if everything you believed was true wasn't?

Very few people on the planet have a matured ego. Most people's egos are immature no matter what physical age they are. This is not good or bad, nor is it to insult anyone anywhere on the planet. This is simply a statement of fact. There are varying degrees of maturity within each ego for example: one person's ego might be 60% mature and another's may be 10% mature, yet another's may be 93% mature. This is simply a process of evolution and no wrongness or failure is involved.

The immature ego is like a 2 to 6-year-old child. It wants what it wants, the way it wants, when it wants it. It is demanding, manipulative, self-centered and often thinks it knows what it's doing. It is the pinnacle of separateness, it is desire to acquire, in many ways it is desire itself. The more it gains or acquires, the more it believes it is real. The more it believes in itself the more it operates the person rather than your consciousness operating the ego.

The ego operates through the use of patterned behaviors. These patterned behaviors determined by and stem from beliefs. Once in these patterns it is difficult for the ego or person to break free of them. When you perceive these beliefs and patterns as your truth they become a prison in which you cannot see beyond the walls. This simply means that you cannot see beyond your limitations and believe the world to be as it is without the ability to imagine, see the possibility of or do something different.

Fear of intimacy or relationships is the ego's fear of the loss of its perceived individuated identity. Since everyone has an ego, it is common for everyone to fear intimacy at some level. At some level every ego fears its demise, unless the person has done inner work to change this perception. If the ego gets too close to anyone, it often experiences not being in charge or experiences a feeling of unity and therefore often feels fearful of the loss of identity. It also fears giving up the concept of separateness, which makes it vulnerable to elimination which isits ultimate fear.

Sometimes the fear of intimacy is the fear of a painful experience based on past relationships.

A committed relationship is one of the best opportunities for a person to grow and often the most threatening for the ego. The relationship could be with another person, their true self or with God/Source. All of these will usually affect the ego the same. Remember that relationships and marriage are geared toward unity and oneness, which in human relationship terms is called intimacy. Hence the fear of intimacy for the average human being.

The concept of marriage and relationships is based on unity.

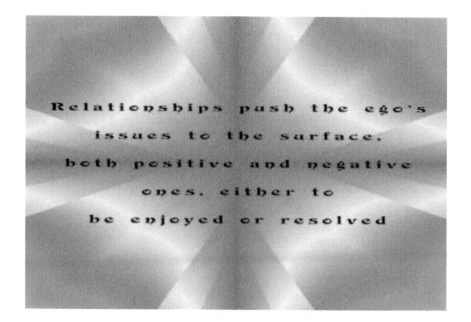

Relationships push the ego's issues to the surface, both positive and negative ones, either to be enjoyed or resolved

Some people will tend to lose themselves in a relationship rather than unify in one, it is usually the person with no sense of self, the belief that they live to serve others or that their own happiness is based on someone else. Relationships push the ego's issues to the surface, positive and negative ones, either to be enjoyed or resolved.

When the ego gets too close to unification of any sort, it will use patterns of behavior to chase the experience or the other person away to avoid its perceived certain death. Remember to the ego, union equals death. When this experience is occurring within a person they may experience unexplainable fear of death or a sense of imminent danger.

A major change in life often feels like you are going to die. The truth is: an old pattern is dying!

The real purpose of the ego is for your soul, your true essence, to experience human existence by using and directing the ego. The ego is a tool for your soul to experience living on earth.

The ego is the navigational software of this world; it is the Windows program, while the personality is the word processing program that interfaces with the world.

Part of your mission in life is to learn how the ego works and then retrain it. Then you will be able to work with it and direct it rather than be governed by it. The next step is then to develop the personality to express your soul/heart's desire.

The higher aspect or consciousness of yourself is the director, your soul is the producer, the ego is the personal experience, and the personality is the expression and actor in the play of life.

Most people never realize this concept. They believe the ego is in charge and often actually think they are the ego. The ego, in fact, is the lower aspect of consciousness of your true self, which means that it is not aware that there is a bigger picture that it is not conscious of.

The Personality

The personality is the means through which the ego maneuvers through life. The personality communicates to other personalities and egos. The ego fulfills its needs on earth through the personality.

The personality is the mask the ego wears to face and interact with the world. The ego is what the soul wears in order to be a human being living on earth.

From birth to early childhood development, the ego learns that it is in charge of the whole show. As a human being grows, a maturation process of the ego is supposed to take place, and when it does the soul or essence of the person begins to take charge of the show.

Simultaneously the personality develops. From parents, family, surroundings and environment the ego develops a belief system that encompasses behaviors, attitudes, perceptions, ideas, etc. which forms the personality.

The personality is often mistaken for the true identity of self.

The personality is the medium for contact with your earthly environment, which includes other people, animals, places and things. Through the personality, behaviors are acted out, feelings and ideas are expressed. Contact with other human beings is managed.

The personality must develop human skills in order to have a fairly enjoyable life. If a person develops excellent human skills, they will most likely have an extremely enjoyable life. With a well-developed personality almost anything is accomplished with a sense of ease. Communication is easily accomplished, and therefore most needs are met fairly easily.

With a poorly developed personality and underdeveloped human skills, life is more than likely going to be difficult and not very pleasant. Communication is tough for the most part and get- ting along with others is difficult at best.

Low Self-Esteem

Low self-esteem occurs when the ego doubts or dislikes the personality it has created. When the ego finds it is not getting what it wants and it sees the personality at fault, it rejects its own creation. The ego then may loathe or despise the personality and wish it to be different or see it as the problem. Once the ego has decided that the personality is flawed, the perception of low self-esteem follows.

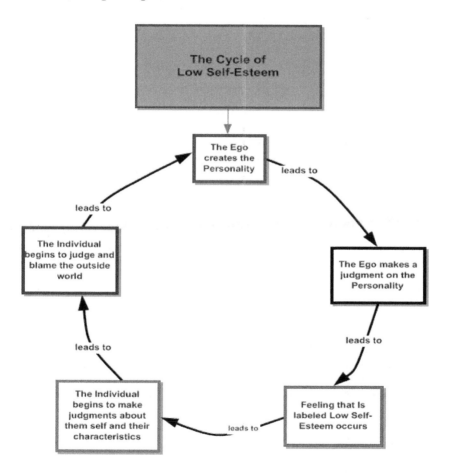

Unbeknownst to the ego, it is the creator of this personality. It has created the best personality it could with the information it had which was the beliefs, thoughts and knowings without the consciousness that it created this flawed personality. And now the ego begins to judge it as flawed and reject the personality. This rejection of the personality is actually the ego rejecting a part of itself.

What actually occurs when this happens is that you decide that a part of you is not good enough or acceptable, and you begin to judge, reject and deny yourself. This is basically making the statement, while creating the assumed personal truth, "I do not love myself." and "I am not good enough."

The rejection of any part of you is an unloving act that creates pain and suffering!

Once the ego believes that the personality is not good enough, it will look for other reasons to criticize itself. Often times the next judgments that occur are about the way you look, your body, your clothes, your intelligence, etc. After that it turns its attention to the outside world and it blames other people or circumstances.

Following this, quite often a person will develop addictions or addictive behaviors such as: eating, weight issues, sex addictions, gambling, substance abuse, etc. These behaviors distract the ego personality from the pain of judgment that t lies within them and focuses on external circumstances to temporarily numb the pain within.

At this point the ego doubts itself and takes on beliefs which block the personality even more. This usually turns into poor social and communication skills, thereby affecting the accomplishment of needs an individual has.

Low self-esteem is only possible for an individual whose soul has not stepped in and gained its matured position. A soul that has done this successfully is what Maslow called 'self-actualized'. This is a soul who is directing the ego with a well-developed personality.

Basic Human Skills
- Survival
- Reproduction
- Basic Communication
- Sense of Self

Masterful Human Skills:
- Inner Self Awareness
- Self-Reflection
- Self-Understanding

- Superb Communication Skills
- Intimacy Skills - with self and other life forms
- Conscious Inner Spiritual Connection
- Conscious Awareness of the Interconnectedness of All Things

Your life is all about you!

The more you understand other people

the more you understand your life!

Know the personality of other people, so as not to be surprised by the behavior. Be aware of their behaviors and try to discern what their real intent is so that you can understand and interact with them. Do not mistake their behaviors for who they really are or what is in their heart. Try to remember that their personality can only respond or react to their circumstances and inner feelings with the limited programs, beliefs and perceptions that they currently have. Often times the person's behaviors do not actually reflect their inner feelings or intent.

The Unconscious

The unconscious is the seat of soul memory, the ego, beliefs, knowings, attitudes and behavior patterning. It is the place that drives a person to behave without thought. It is the 'auto pilot.'

Autopilot is a the place from which you live your life and don't remember how you got where you are and then think life happens to you or that people are doing things to you. The unconscious is the driver for unexplained reactions, behaviors and decisions. It is also the place that controls automatic body functions. From the unconscious all conscious activity and perceptions are influenced or created.

Everything in your life you see, do, and think is influenced by the unconscious. Everything you experience or have experienced ever, in this life or another, is recorded in the unconscious which is connected to and actually part of your soul memory. Soul/unconscious memory brings with you into this lifetime characteristics and traits from previous experiences.

Once a belief is formed and established in the unconscious, the unconscious will seek out ways to confirm and validate this belief then it will seek to manifest the experience of it. The un- conscious will also purposefully avoid or resist anything that challenges your beliefs. The unconscious is not good or bad. Its main purpose is to support the beliefs and knowings, and then create a reality from them at all costs even if that reality is perceived of as negative and creates difficulties and challenges in your life.

Being unconscious is not the same as The Unconscious!

The Conscious is not the same as your conscious awareness!

People think that because they have an awareness about their existence that they are conscious. Most people are living unconsciously while they have a conscious awareness that they are alive.

The unconscious does not judge or make decisions; it only does what it is programmed to do. It does not have the ability of discernment; this is the arena of the conscious mind.

Example: If you believe life is hard and miserable the unconscious will create opportunities for this to be proven. It will attract you to miserable people, endeavors that fail, drive you to decisions that make no sense, hook up with unpleasant partners and whatever events fulfill the beliefs or relative truths it has been given. It does this just because. It has no reasoning, no common sense, no logic. It simply fulfills the beliefs, attitudes and knowings.

The unconscious is not bad, broken or malfunctioning. In fact it is always operating perfectly. It is only the programs, beliefs or knowings that are inaccurate. If the unconscious has been programmed to a state of neutrality and there is space made for your consciousness to direct your

life, life is joyful. When you have made the inner connection within yourself the consciousness of your soul/spirit will be able to direct your life and use the unconscious programs that serve you in a way that creates the life experience you so choose.

*There is no right or wrong, good or bad.
There is only your judgment.*

*There is no right or wrong,
good or bad behaviors.*

*There are only behaviors that you
approve of or disapprove of.*

The Conscious

This is the place where your conscious awareness meets your programs, beliefs, knowings and soul memory. This is the seat of the awareness that where you know you exist. It is the place from which you become aware of things around and within you. This is where free will springs forth into the world.

The conscious mind is where decisions and choices are made. From here you can begin to create anything. The conscious mind overlaps with the unconscious, creating what we call the semi-conscious.

The semi-conscious is where you know what's going on, but it feels like it is a dream and you often forget you did something, but upon reminder and some thought, you kind of remember. It is where people do things they know they shouldn't but do anyway yet can say they didn't do it or do not remember. It is often the land of deception both of self and others.

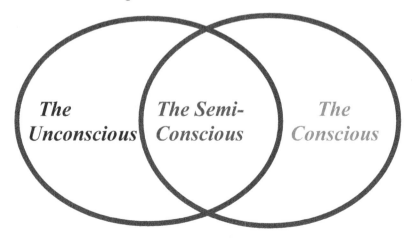

The Unconscious   *The Semi-Conscious*   *The Conscious*

The conscious mind can be developed to a point of maturity where it directs parts of and /or recognizes the patterning of the unconscious. It may grow adept enough to implement enough changes to bring the unconscious into harmony with itself.

Often times the conscious thinks it is more powerful than it is and that it has overcome the unconscious, this is never so.

The conscious mind uses the personality to interact with the world. The conscious mind may further develop the personality until it feels the personality is functional enough.

Once the conscious mind has developed the personality to this point, you must be careful not to fall into a comfortable position and never again pursue further growth. If this should occur, it is likely that old patterns from the unconscious will slowly seep out into the personality and start directing your life in extremely subtle ways.

You must understand that growth never ceases, nor does the expansion of your consciousness. Any time the assumption that you are finished takes hold of your consciousness, you can rest assured you are slowly sliding back into unconsciousness.

Expanded consciousness is not something you have to go to the mountain top to find.

It is with you wherever you are.
All you need is inner stillness and focus
to remember what you have always known
but merely have forgotten.

A conscious human being is aware and present in each and every moment of their life. Although this is a rare experience for a human being to be that conscious all of the time, it is certainly a goal to aim for.

When you become consciously aware in each and every present moment of your life you will find the joy of actually experiencing exactly what you want, although it may not take place in exactly the way you expected. Placing expectations on the way things turn out will certainly be disappointing. Placing your intent and focus on experiencing what you want, in any way that it may turn out, will make the experience enjoyable.

A fully developed consciousness is one that is ever expanding. It has understood how things work in this world. It honors and respects the direction of spirit, and continually recognizes there is always more to learn. It lives in the present, is non-judgmental, is unconditionally accepting and listens to the direction of its higher self (intuition).

The Road to Self-Discovery Never Ends

Integration and Union

One of the greatest challenges in becoming conscious is to gently, lovingly, safely and function- ally integrating the conscious, unconscious, ego, personality and your inner soul spirit into your human experience.

The integration of your divine nature and your own personal human identity allows you to experience being a Divine Human, whereas all the 'negative' qualities of being a human being no longer exist in your life. At this point you can be a

loving, centered creator rather than subject to your patterned behaviors, beliefs, attitudes and knowing.

Truth

The word truth is addressed here because truth is relative to whether it's the ego personality's truth, a conscious or unconscious truth, or an absolute truth of your soul or spirit.

Three types of truth to realize in your life:

1. **Personal truth** - this truth solely affects the ego personality. This is your own personal truth based upon your individual beliefs, thoughts, attitudes, knowings and perceptions. This truth is absolutely unique unto you, although you may find many people that have similar beliefs that to a greater or lesser degree resonate with yours. However each individual's personal truth is absolutely unique unto them and there are no two personal truths exactly alike.

You will often get along better with people who have similar personal truths. Sometimes if your personal truths are too identical or the same, you may even repel or be repelled by those people; but this will depend on the personalities that are involved. A personal truth is an

internal system not necessarily having anything to do with the personality of a person.

2. **Humanity's truth** - this truth is directly related to the conscious and unconscious. This truth directly affects the ego personality's experience.

These are truths that are common to all human beings whether they are conscious of them or not such as: being born, rocks are hard, water is wet, oxygen is required to breathe, I can't fly etc. These truths are also related to what is known as the 'collective unconscious.'

3. **Absolute truth** - this truth is beyond the human experience although they are available to any human being that expands their consciousness. These truths affect both of the previous truths.

These are universal truths that are true throughout all of existence, not just limited to human beings. Human beings are rarely aware of these truths, although they are available to all human beings. This type of truth has been called ancient wisdom, the wisdom of the Masters and Christ consciousness.

Creating Your Life

To create and change your own life, you must decide to do something, anything that is different from what you have already been doing. By this time in your life you should realize that you have a great many limitations, as does everyone. The only way to be free from these limitations is for you to seek freedom.

Things you can do to change your life and manifest your freedom:

- Decide you're going to change.
- Seek out methods to create the changes you want.
- Become aware of your limitations.
- Be aware of limiting thoughts and beliefs.

- Do something to change them!

Without doing something to change your limitations, limiting thoughts and beliefs you are destined to repeat your past or the past of previous generations. Some ideas are available in the book, *The Seven Steps to Freedom.*

Often people believe that knowledge is enough to change their life.

Knowledge is not enough to change your life; Wisdom is required!

Wisdom: *knowledge experienced.*

All too often when someone acquires knowledge, no action is followed; they assume that knowledge is enough for them to change their life. Without that knowledge put into a real-life experience, no wisdom is ever gained.

It would be like believing that because you read about how to change a tire on your car, you have done it. The fact is, you only have the knowledge of how to change a tire; you have yet to experience it by actually changing one. Until you have done it, it is not wisdom that you now have, it is merely knowledge. Knowledge is a great start, but it is by no means the end of the process.

Having this information allows for the opportunity and the understanding to see the importance of becoming aware of how

the ego, personality, conscious and unconscious operate is to you being successful in your life.

Success: experiencing what you enjoy or desire.

Reprogramming your unconscious and training your conscious will allow you to become the wise creator that you truly are.

Love yourself first and foremost, as you can love no other more than you love yourself.

Becoming a wiser creator is a choice and one that you can easily make. Be committed to yourself, you deserve it!

Become a wise creator, experience your knowledge!

Most of all LOVE Yourself!!!

Questions to Get You Started

List beliefs you have about the ego.

List beliefs you have about **your** ego.

What roles do you believe you are? (e.g., mother, teacher, citizen, golfer, a son, a daughter, etc.)

Who do you believe you are supposed to be? (e.g., a good mother, an obedient child, a reliable employee, etc.)

How do you identify yourself? (e.g., rich/poor, pretty/not pretty, honest, dishonest)

Do you need other people to accept you so you feel good?

Do you want to become more conscious?

How much time and effort are you willing to put into your own growth?

Are you ready to do what it takes to be free from what is limiting you?

The ego is the beliefs and perceptions that tell you who you think you are or who you are supposed to be.

In essence your ego is the identity you believe you are.
IT IS NOT WHO YOU ARE.

Section III

Overlays

The Key to Transformation

The Foundation and Basics of Overlays

We are using here the word 'overlays' as the next level of understanding and consciousness that goes beyond beliefs, thoughts, knowings, attitudes, and patterns. Overlays are just that - a layer of consciousness that is laid over a perceived experience. And through those overlays, the perceived experience is interpreted. An overlay uses thoughts, beliefs, knowings, attitudes and soul memory to determine its interpretation of an experience. This section gives an in-depth explanation on how they work and interact.

An overlay is a layer of consciousness that is laid over a perceived experience.

In the beginning, overlays are a way of understanding your experience as a human being. They give you the opportunity to step back from your beliefs and observe them from a different position. Once having understood this and mastered your unconscious overlays, you then have the opportunity to become a creator. As a creator, you may create overlays as a way to interact with people or other beings with a different level of consciousness and perceptions.

From the creator perspective, overlays are tools because they are used consciously to interface with other levels of consciousness and realities. When the overlays are used unconsciously, you are trapped in patterns of behavior associating with energetic fields of influence.

You will automatically process and perceive that which you experience through these filters or overlays. Using the word 'overlays,' is an attempt to describe things from a different level of consciousness that may be more easily perceived and understood as you step back and see your creations as something you have placed over an experience. This is the beginning of a new understanding; and, hopefully, a simpler way to understand that which you are experiencing and assist you in moving forward.

Energetic Overlays - Relationships and Communication

When you feel energetically or you feel the subtleties of the invisible, you know when something has been understood, gotten, received or has been transmitted whether you are conscious of it or not; whether you know how to describe it or not. And since most people don't know how to even discuss this subject matter, it becomes an impossibility to communicate and two people, or more, will get stuck in a cycle of discussion that will seemingly go nowhere.

Now, couple that with your already given behaviors and understandings of each other, this provides for an opportunity for that person to overlay a filter upon the conversation and what happens with the other person, what they are doing, what they are saying, what they mean, what it means to them, what they've seen it mean before and all of their issues associated with the understanding of that type of feeling. Now "I doubly don't get you. I have energetically resisted receiving the information because the moment I have a disagreement my energy field locks up." It becomes non-porous. Now, as the energy field has become non- porous, there is already one layer of wall, so to speak; it is an energy wall.

Overlays blanket communication until all understanding is lost.

Now, if the other person feels that I have not received what they are trying to communicate or that you have not received it, then they will have a wall typically, and their filter will come up and read why your wall or your energy field seized.

Once a person places an overlay on the situation, they are trying to, unconsciously or consciously trap you in it because that overlay wants it to be real. And unless you play a part in it or they can find the right button to push, it is not going to really work. So it's going to kind of frazzle the overlaying, kind of short it out, and then they will want to kind of make that work.

So the auto-fix system in the overlay is going to start covering up, trying to push buttons, seeing little avenues to get you out, little tricks that they know from you, little angles that trigger you so that your emotion will now start to feed into the overlay. So this is basically feed-feeder relationship. And they are feeding with the overlay; and if they can stimulate you into your part of an overlay, then you feed their overlay and then it goes back and forth and it is a symbiotic feeding relationship.

When you are more energetically sensitive, it feels like you are being trapped and you want to just escape. So sometimes the auto-pilot of punching your way out by being aggressive and hostile or retreating and running away are only your only two options because you feel that all that wants to do is to trap you in the overlaying so that you become part of the design.

Now what do we have? What we have is there is an experience of the resistance, a judgment of the resistance, and actually a judgment before the resistance which caused the initial resistance. Then, with that judgment, filters are then applied by all parties; and the resistance is interpreted through multiple facets of which neither party are completely privy to the other person's facets.

So we now have multiple facets upon multiple facets. Now we are trying to understand this and even find a common language to explain and discuss it and it becomes virtually impossible because the refractions off of the resistant energy has becomes so great and so fragmented that it is very hard to gather. And only, we will say, a practiced technician, if you will, knows how to pull that energy back together, read through all of those filters, and come out with some sort of communicative explanation or contact with the other person. Yet if that energy wall is still up and that resistance is still there, there will be the inability to communicate and completely understand each other.

If that energy wall is still up and that resistance is still there, there will be the inability to communicate and completely understand each other.

Couple that with someone being sensitive. In that sensitivity, the person who initiated the conversation may react to the other person to whom they are communicating, who responded with some resistance energetically, all invisible, no words, no gestures, no anything, just the energy of resistance. That person feels that.

Now they have options to respond to that, to see it neutrally and try to communicate beyond it or not. Often times what happens is once the person who was trying to communicate first feels the wall or resistance arise, they have that first encounter which is quite often a little bit of a shock to the energy system especially if you both or all have been in an open space together. So now it shocks the system; there is a little bit of a startle. Upon that startle when the person who has resisted overlays the situation with an energetic interpretation, it is like laying a gray film or

blanket over top of the other person who was trying to communicate.

Once that blanket has been laid over the sensitive person, they have another realization. That first there is resistance energetically to any type of reception of their communication; the second is that they have just been blanketed by an energy field that they cannot get through; not that they are necessarily trapped energetically but they realize that the field between them and the other person is completely impenetrable because that person is having their visions, their judgments, their issues, their interpretations. And then that is backed with the wall of resistance of disagreement and judgments behind that and quite often the person will then surrender conversation.

Or based upon that person's pattern, they may become aggressive and hostile and react because they are in utter frustration at being first resisted, which was a shock to their energy field when they were open; and then feeling the overlay of that energetic interpretation as an entrapment which they want to get out of. So they either fight it or they give in to it and kind of go away on themselves not really being trapped.

Now the problem is that in that communication, once they do either of those, the resistant person now makes more judgments and compounds the situation. And for this example, let's call them the communicator and the resister for now.

Judgments compound the communication problem.

The communicator, once they encounter that shock to their system, if their pattern is to fight and drive their way through it, the resister now will see them as warrior-like and someone they will have to fight against, emotionally, mentally, physically whatever it might be. They will now fight harder and resist them more.

If the communicator then surrenders to the situation and withdraws their communication the person resisting will probably see that as an abandonment or a retreat where they either have to chase them down and attack them to get what they want or seeing that the communicator has abandoned the relationship or the communication, abandon it themselves.

So, in a way, once the resister has resisted, there is a challenged at best; but once the resister has put an overlay of interpretation energetically on the situation, it is nearly impossible to complete a communication and get a thorough understanding because it has been so distorted that it can't even be cleared up until the resister at least takes the overlay off.

If a communicator pushes against and feels the energetic charge of the one resisting, the communicator could themselves resist also and now there is dual resistance. Upon that, both the communicator and the resister can place even another overlay over the double resistance. And you have a double resistant, double overlay.

Remember, the only thing a resister resists is the interpretation of the energy they feel. In most cases, it's never about the circumstances or the words themselves. It is the perceived energy experience when the words are said or spoken. It could be combined with a gesture, a look, a movement, a position, any of those things could be combined; but remember all of those things are energetic in nature. So the resister sees, feels, experiences, sensates; they feel that energy energetically coming from the communicator and that is what causes the resistance.

Once the resistance occurs and an overlay is placed, all logic is typically lost from the conversation. And it becomes an emotionally charged, overlaid conversation that usually ends up going nowhere, long and drawn out, painfully and energetically exhausting until everybody surrenders or gives up their resistance and removes the overlays.

When the overlay is removed by the resister, there is the possibility of talking through the resistance much like you would talk over the fence rather than hug. And then the resister has the option to take down the wall, no fence, openly receiving the information and then the possibility of understanding takes place.

This is all energetic; it is all invisible; it is often not done by words; and people who don't understand, feel, or see these things will get caught in the argument of circumstances and stories and try to prove themselves or evidence themselves and maybe even pretend like none of that took place by saying "I don't know what you are talking about, I didn't say anything that way, I don't know what you mean; that is not what I intended." And all the invisible takes place while both parties intuitively know that this is going on but no one can consciously come to the awareness that this is what is happening and that this is really what the problem is.

Only when resistance ends is there the possibility for communication.

That is all the problem is: that a resister meets resistance or a communicator meets resistance or an overlay is placed on the original resistance. And once that overlay takes place, the whole thing becomes almost impossibly distorted until you can talk the resister down, so to speak, from their overlay.

For a marker for you, overlays are quite often displayed through an emotional response. Resistance may or may not be shown as an emotional response. It depends upon the individual; how controlled they are; how manipulative they are, etc. But once the emotions start to come out, it is evident that an overlay has taken place. For now, we will just describe it as an energetic overlay. Reminding you that quite often what happens is that there is resistance, then an energetic overlay and then a total disconnect in whatever the relationship is.

Energetic Overlays - The Communicator

We are using a new languaging system and we are speaking from an energetic perspective about patterns, beliefs, behaviors and attitudes. So we are introducing a different level of understanding to see this that these are energetic in their nature rather than beliefs based in their nature.

Remember that when we are talking communicator, resister and we are talking about the overlays that if you are the communicator and you walk in with an attitude, an idea, or preconception of the person or people who you are talking to, then you have already begun the conversation with an overlay. So you may be the original overlay before they even became a resister in a communication with you.

If you've got an attitude, idea or preconception - you've got an overlay!

So you have to re-evaluate and double check once you see the resistance. Were you actually the initial overlay that caused the resister to respond? If not, then you move forward. If so, then you have to remove your overlay from the conversation or communication so that it will allow the resister to stop resisting because they initially felt your overlay walk into the conversation and responded to it intuitively. And then every word that you said after that was coming through both of your filters and the communication just decays.

With energetic overlays, you can see the human understanding of them might be expectations; but expectations still don't quite describe an overlay. But you can see how your overlays can possibly be interpreted as expectations because when you place that overlay or that blanket over the experience and you now look at it, you are expecting to see it a certain way; expecting to experience it a certain way. And so with those overlays, you now distort any type of present experience and it is all based upon the past.

And you could have potentially multiple overlays that just cloud the layers even more with the distortions which do not allow you to truly experience any given moment or truly see another individual for who they are because your overlay already tells you what they should act like, be like, how they will respond and what you want from them. This does not allow the other individual to truly express themselves to you only because you won't be able to hear them.

So they may truly express themselves but no matter what they say, it will be limited to what you are allowing to come through your overlay or your filters. So you can see how this would be expectation - because somewhere unconsciously you are going to see them the way you are going to see them and they really can't do anything about it.

This is another perspective of how you can only be responsible for yourself and the way you say or do things. You can't be responsible for how other people interpret them. It goes back to the basics and The Concepts. And so you stay in your present moment as filterless as possible, as pure or as without overlays as possible and you express from your position in the best and the most appropriate way you know how. That is all you can do when interacting with others. The rest is up to them, they must choose to take away their overlays.

So you have two people standing overlay-free being able to see each other clearly. And then once they see clearly, it is to look at them without judgment. Because even if you pull back your overlay, you may still be waiting to overlay what they say or do with a judgment. Now if you can do this, overlay-free, without going into judgment and waiting to put that overlay on an encounter, you are able to unconditionally accept another which allows you to see who they really are. Sure, you will see their personality and their ego structure, but you will also really be able to see who they are, their essence.

*You must be unconditionally accepting
to see who the other person really is.*

And then knowing each other's ego personality structure, you know how to speak to each other; you know how each other's patterns will respond; and you can do the best you can to speak in their language so that you can actually connect with their essence from the human individuated experience which allows for real connection at a human level.

And part of what overlay-free would look like would be to be mindless; to be thoughtless, as we have spoken about before, without thought, without mind, simply and purely with awareness. What we are explaining with the overlays is just another way to understand what is going on that will reach another part of you, a different understanding with you to assist you. But ultimately it covers much of the same stuff we have been speaking about for years - mindlessness, thoughtlessness, without thought, without mind.

To be thoughtless is to be overlay free.

In that space it also makes room for the heart to have a pure experience. And in the pure experience of the heart is pure awareness. With the pure awareness, you have the capability of using your human skills to decide if or what needs to be done or responded to. But the key is thoughtlessness or mindlessness with an open heart coming from pure awareness. In that state, you are overlay-free.

In the pure experience of the heart is pure awareness.

Overlays - Yours, Mine and Theirs

When two people are in an overlay together, there is no conversation. There are only two overlays or more, combating for position to see who will have the predominant overlay and convince the other person that their overlay isn't as important, as strong or as right as your overlay so that the other person can be in agreement with your overlay. And whoever argues the best, holds out the longest usually gets the overlay 'win.' Not that they ever really win anything, but they get to perceive they have won. And all they won was the right to have other people involved in their overlay.

The distortion is that if you project your overlay stronger, more potently, bigger, better, more colorful somehow your overlay will be accepted as the winning overlay, and everybody will see the world the way you do. The problem is that even if someone accepts your overlay and you have the illusion of winning the overlay perception, they are still having their own overlay within yours; so they don't even see yours the way you want them to see it anyway.

So you still don't get your way even though you thought and had the illusion you won. It is however a great illusion. And you get to walk away thinking you won something; and everybody saw it your way; or somebody saw it your way; and still have no idea that they don't. They are still viewing through their overlay within your overlay and it is still not the same.

The deal to understand is that no two overlays are ever the same, nor can anyone be absorbed by your overlay. They can only agree to play it the way you like to from their overlay. So there is an agreement upon a common playing ground but there is never an absorption into your overlay or the way you see the world.

No one but you sees your overlay.

And to add, a creator could allow someone to have their overlay and still choose to participate in it because they want the experience or don't mind the experience or really have no care about the experience. And they are just saying "Okay have your overlay. It's great. Let's enjoy it; let's do it; let's see what it is like. Let's have a blast." Say "Oh you have an overlay, let's do it. I don't feel like making one up; I will follow yours. I have no care which one. Let me see how you experience the world; this could be fun or interesting." That would be a conscious choice to participate in someone else's overlay with an overlay of your own. Because remember you have to have an overlay in order to interface with someone else's overlay even if your overlay is "Hey, I am going to participate with you." It allows you a common ground to communicate from and have a co-experience.

Overlays - Past and Present

The Energetic Fields of Influence are what the overlays are made of. It is the material that is woven into the blanket of the overlay. Your beliefs are the sewers or the stitchers using the Energetic Fields of Influence that you weave your overlay with. Now, that is this lifetime; what you know about this lifetime.

Now we are going to talk about bringing it from other places. Overlays are brought with you on your journey. It is what once we may have called your energetic backpack, your soul memory, your other life experiences, whatever you want to call it. It is the patterning or the fabric that you carry around with you and throw over your experiences in order to read them, make sense of them, make order of them, etc.

*Overlays are the patterning or fabric
that you carry around with you
and throw over your experiences
in order to make sense of them.*

In general, the overlays that we are talking about are overlays that interfere with your clarity. These overlays could be from some other planetary system. It could be from some other non-physical experience. Now you bring in these overlays and they influence the perceptions of your overlays in whatever individuated experience you are having. In part these overlays are also things that you have chosen, at some level, to clear, clarify, or resolve, or experience.

In any particular lifetime, you have multiple upon multiple overlaid potentials. Just for a given experience and an example, let us say that you had a million lifetimes. Well you have a million plus combinations of overlays that you are bringing through in any giving experience based upon the frequency or consciousness that that individuated manifestation of you is able to process or experience, because some of the overlays may be at too dense a frequency for you to process or too light or high of frequencies for you to process in the particular embodiment you are in.

As you have taken this lifetime in your human form, you are here to process as many of those overlays as possible. It is not even process. So we are using inaccurate words. Maybe we need to say, you are here to resolve your lack of clarity and these overlays now are being brought to the forefront so that you can clear up your vision as much as possible. And in clearing up your vision, what we are also saying is that you are creating a wisdom or a consciousness that is much clearer, that can travel multi-dimensionally without having to be clutter with all of this what we will call 'baggage of overlays.'

So in a given lifetime, in particular people who are attempting to do what you are doing, you are clearing as much as possible multiple overlays from multiple times and places for the acceleration of the consciousness for your integrated spirit and human experience. This is your acceleration. This is what people would call your ascension. What we would just say is an expansion of your consciousness in your embodied forms because ultimately your spirit is all of that expanded consciousness but in an embodied form of whatever type of density.

Your spirit is not a master of it until it manifests an aspect of itself, or you, into that realm to have the experience of that realm. For example, an angel having never been a human being will not have a clue as to how to be a human being. It will seem like a mystery school, like it is really a mystery. They will not know how to function. They will interpret things inaccurately. They won't be able to figure out programs they get as a human being and they will be fundamentally distorted. Then it will be challenging for them to experience their human life. This is what someone would call a 'young soul.'

An old soul, who has traveled and experienced the overlays, and their spirit has embodied in the human form before, will have the records and the remembrances of all their experiences in order to access and integrate that with their current human experience patterns, programs and overlays.

So now where we want to expand you to is to recognize that many of your overlays are not from this lifetime, as we would refer to it. Lifetime is not exactly an accurate description of travel. It is a way for human beings to communicate that there is an experience beyond this experience. So they talk about this like you have had multiple lifetimes. But, in truth, you are just life itself experiencing multiple experiences. They are not truly just lifetimes.

Many of your overlays are not from this lifetime.

So as you travel and have these multiple experiences, as you have traveled across the universes, through the galaxies, through the dimensions, through the levels of consciousness, whatever metaphor you want to use for this type of description because this is very hard to explain in human terms. We can actually describe this in a sensible fashion to most of you. And for those who haven't done any, we will call it, 'homework', then this languaging will be totally way out there or not understood.

At the same time, there may be these young people, as you would see them, come in and understand this languaging completely because they are so already attuned to this information. And they are not coming in as veiled with as many overlays as those before them have brought. So now when you have your daily life experience as a human being, it is wise for you to remember that your overlays are not just from this lifetime. But see how these overlays are the blankets which you place over life and you see your experience of the human life through. Some of it may not make any sense. With some of the overlays you may not even know why you are doing them, why you repeat them, or why you continue them. In truth, none of that matters.

When you reach a place of a certain awareness, all you need to do is understand the essence of what the overlay is. When you understand the essence of what the overlay is you just basically flip the switch off and that illusion dissipates, then you are able to see clearly. You do not need to process intensely; you do not need to go through it.

*When you understand the essence of the overlay
you basically just flip the switch off and that
illusion dissipates,
then you are able to see clearly.*

This is a completely different level of consciousness and awareness that both you are experiencing and that you are bringing availability of to the planet for those after you to experience much quicker than has ever been able to have been done before by the general population. So the younger kids will be able to access this information, flip the switch in a heartbeat, and they don't have to do what you have done for years to overcome your challenges and finally get to this place of this awareness.

In your freedom, you set the pace for freedom for all that come here to experience. We are truly explorers when we manifest. You are truly creators when you manifest. And you blaze a trail, behind you, you leave a vast open potential of consciousness that anyone can take in any direction they so choose.

YOU blaze a trail for others
and open a vast potential of consciousness!

And in doing this, all of the changes that are about to come in the next five years, will seem astounding in many ways. Many will be slow to leak out because they are withholding the information, trying to hold on to the old patterning. But there are astounding discoveries that are coming, that are already taking place, that have yet to hit the common consciousness. And because you and others like you have blazed the trail, you have left an open space for others to adventure and create.

So, in your own journey, you have provided a great service for all those who will come after you in this dimension. Understand that it gets quite easier as you go if you do your homework, so to speak. If you pay attention to yourself, if you create your own awareness, if you step forward into your journey, you will find that you will be able to run and you won't even have to move your legs. That is how quickly the acceleration will take place.

Things that you discover will also at the same time seem like, "Oh, I already know this." because you do. In many ways, it is not going to be new. And in many ways it is going to be new - very strange position. Yes, it is new to your conscious awareness and your experience as a human being coming from the limitations that you have placed upon yourself, that you have been born into, that were created by the general conscious of planetary experience.

And so as you realize this, you will find that everything will move quicker. Stop holding onto the idea that you have to process, work hard at, or do something, and yet you have to do something. And part of this is just letting go of your old consciousness, stopping the habits, addressing any beliefs or patterns that still may exist within your overlays.

Stop holding onto the idea that you have to process,
work hard at or do something.

Remember, the overlay is what we are referring to as the whole blanket if you will. A pattern is the design within the blanket. Many multiple patterns create the weaving of that blanket that we are calling an overlay. And in those patterns are the energetic fields of influence, thoughts, beliefs, knowings, and attitudes. All those are what make up the fabric or should we say, the yarn that is used to weave the patterns within the overlay.

And so we have fundamentally begun by breaking down the thoughts, beliefs, knowings, attitudes to a form of understanding and the ability to change them. This then changes the yarn that you are weaving the new patterns with while we take down the old patterns and remove the blanket to where there is no blanket. And the new pattern woven is the pattern of clarity of pure vision, of pure understanding with the ability to create freely without limitation of the thoughts, beliefs, knowings, attitudes, patterns and overlays.

It is the beginning of your freedom experienced. And up until this point, you have not had the freedom that you are about to experience. It is for you to be conscious of not repeating your habits, your old thoughts, your old understanding. Simply by doing that you will create an illusion of an overlay of which you can perceive the illusion is real and then perceive through the false overlay and create an experience that does not exist. So now it is to catch yourselves when you are creating or fabricating stories without clarity or acting or asking questions.

In the case of functionality, how would you do whatever you believe you are perceiving, in order to check that it is a clear reality? Whether it is yours or someone else's or both, you must, as the human being, ask questions. You must be a detective to discover is what you are believe you are perceiving clarity or an overlay that is or isn't real? That is what the functional piece of this process will look like.

You will be able to do this with family, friends, associates and children. You should be able to ask these questions. And even if someone is not receptive to these questions, you will ask them in a way that you will find out what the truth is for you. And then you will be able to discern; are you perceiving a reality that is yours? Or are you perceiving a reality that is theirs or someone else's? Then you will be able to discern which reality it is; and you will be able to place yourself in a position of clarity, if you so choose.

Is this my reality?

For example, if you are looking at someone else's pattern, you are interacting with someone else, you cannot determine whether it is an overlay of yours or theirs. You can ask them questions to see how they are experiencing this interaction with you. Then you will check within yourself to see if you agree with this experience. And you will discern the difference between whether it is an internal experience or an external agreed upon experience.

For example, you are both pushing on a door. Are you experiencing that internally and are you physically doing it outside? You may be physically doing it outside and not experiencing it inside. Then is it truly your reality? Not necessarily. If you are speaking to someone and you are talking about a coffee can; and they see the coffee can and they say the coffee can is red, it's cold, it's ugly, it's beautiful. And you are looking at the coffee can and you are having no internal judgment about this. You are simply observing the coffee can. There is no feeling of it being ugly, beautiful, or hot, or cold, or anything. It is just a coffee can. In that case you may be observing someone else's reality. And you do not have to believe it or take it on as your own experience.

If someone is angry, you will ask certain questions, observe physical behaviors; and then check within you to determine if you are actually angry, if you are feeling responsible for the anger, if you feel you need to take on the anger. And then you would determine that, let us say, in this case, "No I do not. I don't need to take it on. It is not mine. I am not truly upset. And it is actually their experience and I am feeling them in their reality. I am able to say that it isn't my reality although I am observing their reality. And I can recognize that I do not have a personal overlay on this nor am I vested in this."

If, in that same angry case, you were feeling responsible for them, or you were feeling the need to change it for them, that would be a case of you having an overlay and believing that reality was yours and thereby interconnecting with their reality through a common overlay.

So with these understandings, you will be able to discern your experiences differently. You will be able to understand the difference between a common perceived reality, a common reality where you are both experiencing the exact same thing or the experience of observing someone else's perceive reality or overlay. This allows you to be a creator.

This discernment allows you to step clearly into your own field and decide what you wish to create or experience. As opposed to being drawn into actions or decisions based upon an overlay you have placed on a situation and responded to that overlay through patterned behaviors and energetic fields of influence such as anger, guilt, shame, grief, whatever they may be. See how this new perception actually sets you free from so many limiting, constrained systems and ways that you have previously perceived the world and believe it to be. This is the beginning of your freedom.

We are also looking at these overlays as if they are blanket you are watching from a distance that you have thrown over top of an experience. So the idea that you are consciousness has shifted you from being in the Energetic Field of Influence and trying to stop them or being in a belief and trying to stop it to you standing and throwing the blanket over the physical world that you are looking at and you watching the blanket and what how that blanket changes the picture. This place is a place of discernment now. It sets you free.

The place of discernment sets you free.

And from that place, with the new energetics that you are receiving and assimilating, you can weave that new vision of clarity while you continue to just dissipate the old overlays,

patterns, and the yarn you have woven that blanket pattern with. It is freedom at a different place.

And now, once you are able to undo these overlays, which is done in a heartbeat, even though we are making it sound like it is long and arduous maybe, we are not really undoing; it is instantly done. All it takes is a shift of your consciousness and awareness of what you are doing and a change in your behaviors, attitudes, and habits; and it will instantly change. You will experience everything completely different in a heartbeat if you able to do that.

And understand it will probably take you practice. It is not like you will do it overnight. That practice will get quicker and quicker and the awareness will get quicker and quicker, much faster than anything that you have done to date, for many reasons. Because you have done your own work; because the energy that is available on the planet and the consciousness that is available vibrates at a higher frequency that allows this to be done. So here you are at this miraculous time of shifting of consciousness that things are going to change so quickly that it will be amazing.

With practice the awareness will get quicker and quicker, much faster
than anything that you have done to date.

What seemed to occur in the last century that was so much more advanced and quickly accelerated compared to centuries before, you will see a doubling in those changes in this century. Things that were believed impossible, such as it was impossible to fly, such things as teleportation, or technology that transports you from one place to another will be seen by the end of this century. The ability to move consciously from your own consciousness will be available to some. The ability to create with just consciousness physical things will be seen in this century.

What may have been called "miracles" will come to be commonplace as it had done in the last century, but the acceleration is at least double. So it will be your experience as you start to see more of these overlays.

Now understand and remember that you have overlays from the other experiences of life. And with those overlays, you have to remember that sometimes you may confuse them with current day overlays and then have a distorted perception. So it is to keep in mind that if something makes absolutely no sense about what the overlay looks like in this lifetime that it is probably related to multiple life experiences that are being confused. And all you need to do is find the essence of that overlay and flip the switch, if you will; and clarity will arrive. And it can be done in a heartbeat.

Patterning Explained

Knowing that overlays are woven together with the Energetic Fields of Influence, forming patterns, these overlays create a film or a perceptual reality that your consciousness, when hyper-focusing on the overlay, forgets itself. It loses consciousness and then it begins to believe the overlay. And then, after it believes in the overlay, it begins to make decisions and judgments based upon the belief in the overlay, all the while you are forgetting who you really are and believing the overlays and identifying with the overlays, losing consciousness, actually having lost consciousness of yourself, your true essence. You believed in the identities of the overlays charged with the patterns and energetic fields of influence and began to live a life that wasn't even yours. But you believed it was because you forgot who you were. You lost consciousness.

When you believe the overlay
you are lost in the illusion.

A metaphor would be when you sit at a computer screen. You are so hyper focused on the computer screen and what is on it, that you forget about the world around you, that you are actually the operator of the computer. And you begin to believe that you are what is on the screen. And now you have lost consciousness and you are in the world of the computer and you forgot who you are - the operator sitting in the chair, observing the screen, making the mouse and keyboard do as you want. But when you are so completely lost in the computer screen, you are not even aware that your hand is moving the mouse or typing on the keys. You just see it occurring on the screen and the screen becomes the reality.

That is what it is like when you become unconscious or believe in the illusion of the human world or any other world for that matter.

Overlays and Distortions

Through all the history of earth, there have been many distortions and corruptions. It is why it has sunk so low into density as it did. And those distortions come through many ways; maybe you were a whale or a dolphin and they were doing experiments on the whales and dolphins whether they were what people would call ETs, or whether they were human beings.

When they were doing genetic experiments in Atlantis, when they were fusing together and joining different creatures and blending animals and humans, all of these distortions took place. All of these left memories in the earth's eco system if you will as well as the beings that travel here, which in this case a lot of you did.

And so those distortions placed a lot of fear, a lot of pain, a lot of misunderstandings. Some of you were the experimenters and the experimentees in many lifetimes, in many positions, both good and bad, light and dark as it would be labeled as a human being. But really good and bad, light and dark were just experiencing both aspects of the polarity because this is a polarized universe. And in that polarity, in order to master it, you had to get it; had to experience both poles or you could not be a master. A master does not only experience one half of an experience that it likes to experience; it experiences everything or to some degree or aspect of it in order to know it as its own. To be the master, you must have the experiential wisdom in one way or another.

So it is to remember that in all of your experiences and all of your distortions, you did nothing wrong. You were simply having experiences. And when you had those experiences, unfortunately or fortunately, those experiences stuck as realities and truths because you made judgments on them. And once you made the judgment, you anchored them with you and then you carried them and then saw all of your future experiences through those overlays, those overlays of judgments.

You did nothing wrong - you were simply having experiences.

And really if we were going to summarize it, all an overlay is a blanket of judgment. This is why we have said to you that if you are judgment free, you are free. The only way to be pain free is to be judgment free. And the only way to be judgment free is to cease judgment of self and self's experience whether it is the human self or the soul self. When you cease all of judgment of self at all levels, you are judgment free and you are no longer connected to those overlays thereby changing your experience of every experience.

The only way to be free is to stop judging self.

And in that freedom, it allows you to create within each experience whatever you want to perceive. Creation is the creation of perception. You are creating perceptions. How else could you come into a world of illusions and have any experience if it wasn't a perception? So you create perceptions. You create experiences. Or we could say you create experiential perceptions.

And if you are clear and free from these overlays, you can create any experiential perception you want to and know that it is a creation, not get lost in it or sucked into it, and simply play with it. It

is where the fun comes in. You create an experiential perception to play with, not to become, not to form an identity, not to make judgments but simply to have the experience.

And once, or as you get freer of your overlays, the experiential perceptions that you create will become more fun, more enjoyable, less tedious, less difficult. And so we go to the place of enjoyment of your embodiment as a creator, a creator of the experiential perceptions.

Conscious and Unconscious Overlays

Switching from conscious to unconscious overlay, back and forth, creates some of the difficulties and transitional problems you are having in your body and having with other people; and understanding it all. Also, some difficulties you are having within yourself about understanding it or translating it or even assimilating it. It is a little odd. It is like back and forth, back and forth, back and forth. "Okay, I am a little dizzy. Which one am I in? I just changed so quickly that I don't remember which one I am in. Let me get orientated here. Oh yeah, here I am. Oh I don't want to be over here. Oh let me go back to this one." And it takes a little bit for the personality and the ego to catch up so it gets used to the fluctuation.

This is what inter-dimensional travel would be like. You are travelling from one dimensional frequency to another; and if your body, personality and ego haven't adjusted to that kind of travel, it is like traveling at light speed and it takes a little time for you to catch up. All of your particles are not in the same place at the same.

But when you go through this and you are traveling inter-dimensionally and you are actually holding a form, no one outside of you will probably notice that anything has changed at all. And if they do, again it will just be "Oh you look different. You feel different. There is something different about you. I don't know what it is and I can't put my finger on it."

And yet you are having a completely different internal experience than you ever did before; but because you have kept the human overlay so that you could interface with the human world, you will look sort of the same; you will behave sort of the same; you will have some of the same experiences; and you will have overlapping human experiences and traits in order to be able to interface with the human world. That is just part of the process.

If your body, personality and ego haven't adjusted to that kind of travel,
it is like traveling at light speed
and it takes a little time for you to catch up.

Acclimating internally to this change is the challenge. It is not particularly noticeable except by someone who has sight. We don't mean visualize sight. We mean inner sight where they can actually see, feel and hear that which is not seen. They will notice something is different. Now depending on their level of awareness, they will either put a finger on it or just be able to say, "Hey, I see this is happening." That is pretty common. So understanding this is very helpful to you, your human, your ego personality so you can manage this shifting reality.

Understanding these things is an important aspect to changes to elevated consciousness. If not, this could be drastically devastating to the ego personality and your experience here. It could literally short out your personality. You would recover but you would come back really disoriented and it would take quite some time. A few people get that kind of zap and it has taken them years to re-acclimate and settle down. That could literally destroy everything that you are experiencing because let's say, circumstantially, you could lose your job, lose your family, lose a relationship that you really enjoyed. All those things could just take place and then make it more challenging upon re-entry.

So you want to make the exit and re-entry process if you will, more comfortable, as easy and as comfortable as possible. So, in this time that we are in, as the perception goes, this takes a little bit of a process. And so it is being patience but it also understanding these shifts.

When you finally decide to make the shift into creator, it is a bit disorienting at times to the identity you believe you are holding. So if you are the identity of Sam who is going through these changes, that identity is going to have some disorientation. All the programs and patterns will come up that will add to the complications. And as the morphing takes place (understanding that it is morphing rather than illness and death) it is going to disorient Sam's personality and identity also.

When you finally decide to make the shift into creator, it is a bit disorienting at times to the identity you believe you are holding.

So it takes a little practice; it takes a little patience; and most of all, it takes some tolerance of your experience. But knowing that once you get to the other side, so to speak, you will be in the creator seat; and you will be creating overlays so that you can interface in any situation that you would like to interface. And each one of you has a message, has a skill, has a purpose in your own way; and you will each want to interface with particular levels of consciousness and realities.

And through that you will transmit your wisdom simply by your presence. This is what a master does. A master doesn't literally sit and teach. A master interfaces with other realities; and through that master's presence, the energy and information of their wisdom is just transmitted and received.

> *Through that master's presence, the energy and*
> *information of their wisdom*
> *is just transmitted and received.*

Understanding Interactive Overlays

We are trying to bring in higher frequencies to the world with the consciousness that it is at. And with those higher frequencies, in order for them to interact and affect this realm, there has to be an interactive overlay.

So with an organization for children with invisible challenges, what has to happen is that they have to create a sense of what is perceived of as normalcy; and through that normalcy, communicate the higher consciousness. So that through that interactive overlay, the average human being can receive those frequencies in a way that is palatable; that doesn't change who they are as far as the personality. We are not making you give up everything. We are just saying, "Oh, here is the way you make change to make greater comfort and creation in your life." And it goes through that overlay.

And that overlay allows for the choice of those beings in the human world to decide if they want that higher frequency or not. Do they want to make the shift or not? Then they can choose to interact with the organizations' overlay and the transmission will take place. The organization will then walk away and those people will have the information they need for the rest of their journey.

It is the same with anything you do. You will have the frequency that you have brought in; that you have acquired through your own growth and stepping into the creatorship. Someone will spot it and say, "Oh, I want something like that." And in order for them to have the opportunity to wake up, there needs to be an interactive overlay through which communication is possible. Through that interface, they will be able to receive the energy information and even words that they need for their own expansion and growth.
And once that has taken place, to whatever degree it is going to, whether it is one time or multiple times, then the overlay is no longer necessary. The creator can dissolve that overlay and never interact with that consciousness, being or entity, ever again if they so choose.

But what is added is that once having connected to that being or consciousness, the availability of dialing that number, so to speak, is always at hand. Because the interface has already been made; there has been a connection; there is sort of a knowing between both; and it can be dialed up by either party. And you, as the transmitter of information, can decide if you want to answer the call or make a call.

Just because you have made a connection with someone through the holographic overlay that you have created, doesn't mean that you have to continue it or answer it even if they call up on it. You have the option as the creator to say, "No, finished that overlay. I don't really need that interactive communication any longer. I am not going back there." or "Oh, I will take the call; let's see what they want today."

And now it is you designing the overlay that you are going to have to interface with whatever level of consciousness you are choosing to experience.

Being a Creator - Beliefs and the Matrix

The problem with the whole belief system idea is that, in most cases, you are in the beliefs, you are not observing them. It is the attitude, "I have a belief." "I have an identity." "I have to process." "I have to ..." And the "I am" ("I have") statements are the claiming of it being yours or the claiming of you. "I have belief systems. It's my thoughts. It's my attitudes. It's my beliefs." These statements are proof you are in the belief system.

When you move to the place of the overlays, it allows you to recognize you believed you had them. Notice, you believed you had them. And now you can see how you were believing your beliefs because now you have stepped into an observer position and recognized these as overlays. And the explanation that we gave you in regards to the 'losing your consciousness,' shows you how you just kind of fell asleep. You saw it, you stared at it so long, you thought it was you, you believed it was you, you went into it and wow, it became a reality and now you have the beliefs associated with that reality.

Now in order to get out I have to undo my beliefs. Many people believe and chase after the idea that all I have to do is find that one core belief and all of the sudden I will be enlightened. My whole world will change if I get that belief or those two or three beliefs. I believe that this is true. Well, now, I am still in the belief system.

By moving to this next degree of understanding, you can see what the overlays are because your perceptions have changed. At this level of understanding you get that the overlays are made up of those beliefs, your beliefs. You can see that your thoughts, beliefs, attitudes, knowings and patterns actually are what make or create the overlay.

Your thoughts, beliefs, attitudes,
knowings and patterns
actually are what make or create the overlay.

Now theoretically, once you really become a true observer and step beyond the overlay and out of the patterns, thoughts, beliefs, knowings, attitudes, etc., once you step out of that, you can stand back as the creator and move those around. Sort of like a touch screen computer, you can move them around, shift them, and have a different perceptual experience knowing that you are having a different perceptual experience because you moved them around. That is a whole different level of creatorship.

While you are stuck in the overlay, and another way to view it possibly or explain it, is that the overlay is the matrix, the accepted limited model of life designed to keep you limited, the 'norm.' But it is a self-imposed, self-created overlay; something that you believe in. That is what the matrix is. As long as you are in the matrix or the overlay as a truth, then you are subject to everything that goes on and is connected to it. It is a giant circuitry. If you step out of the overlay, you step out of the matrix and you can play with it any way you like, and then it becomes fun. Then it is a whole different ball game.

In order to get to that creator position, you had to willingly and consciously give up your attachment to the overlays and the matrix. Without your conscious choice and willingness, you are still attached to the circuitry, and subject to what goes on. Oh you might be less connected,

but you are still connected. The only true freedom is complete and total separation from that overlay/matrix design. And then in that freedom, you can visit it just for the fun of it.

As long as you are attached you are trapped in the illusion.

Creator Overlay

A creator will create an overlay that they are conscious of, that they are using to interface with another level of consciousness or another level of perception. So they recognize what that level of perception is; they create an overlay, a system, a look, a behavior, a persona, whatever you want it to be; they create that in order to be able to interface with that other level of existence. That overlay is now a creator overlay, not an autopilot, not a systematic, not an old memory; this is now a creator overlay.

Creating an overlay consciously is being a creator.

In order to interface with the world of form, you have to have some sort or semblance of form or else you couldn't be seen; or else you couldn't interact; or else you couldn't experience. So you have to create an overlay that you can take and place over top of that existence that has enough similarities so that there is an interactive joining. With that overlay, the beings in that particular level of perception that you are trying to interact with can see you and experience you. That allows for interactive experience.

So you create a persona that can interact with other human beings that is at a vibratory level through which those other beings can see, feel and experience this persona. This, for our discussion, we will call a creator's interactive overlay where it is directed, manifested, and transformed as the creator sees fit or needs to transform in order to have the interactive experience or effect on that level of perception that they want to have or to experience.

So in order for you to participate with other human beings, first of all, typically what has happened was that you are born as a human, believed you were a human being, got lost in your humanity and believed that was who you were. That was a way to instantly merge with that reality and have the experience of that reality in order to gain your own wisdoms and experience because the purpose of that was for you and your experience only.

Now as you go to the remembrance of self, you start to step away. How did we begin to do this in your journey? You began by understanding beliefs, thoughts, understanding, creations, ego personality. This all started to break down the idea that you were this identity. It began to open up space for your spirit to come in and allow that to have a creator's interactive overlaid experience. Awful wordy but it is really what has happened.

And the more conscious you become, the more you step away from the belief systems, patterns, and the unconscious overlays, or the soul memory, or karmic overlays as you might call them. So as you step away from them, there is a detachment; and in that detachment, the persona that you have created has challenges with understanding what to do and feel with this new experience because it is like popping out of something but then trying to re-orient because you are kind of dizzy.

Well there is a literal type of dizziness and that dizziness is when your energetic fields or your bubble begins to spin. When you bubble begins to spin, it is the beginning of infusing your human experience with consciousness. So you may experience dizziness, nausea, aches and pains, all kinds of things; any kind of symptom that you can imagine a human being might experience from the place where you believed you were a human being.

So from the human perspective, all of those aches and pains would be labeled as illness, disease, something is wrong. And so from that level consciousness, you are searching for something that is wrong because it means something bad is going to happen. It is a polarized perspective without understanding.

Now once you step out of that karmic or soul memory overlay system into consciousness, you realize that these aches and pains are about morphing. The aches and pains are about turning on your light bodies, your energy bodies, your consciousness. And it is part of the detachment from the overlays.

So it is sort of that detaching from your human consciousness and those unconscious overlays is perceived of as painful. So it sort of hurts. So now without looking at this from a greater perspective, you will assume that these hurts equal human's understanding of pain, disease, illness, etc. When in truth many people are simply detaching from those unconscious overlays. And the detachment means that the bodies are lightening literally, that the light bodies are turning on and so it sort of hurts. It is like when your leg or arm falls asleep, and it begins to wake up and you have needles and pins. It is the same idea.

Detachment from overlays means
that the bodies are lightening literally,
that the light bodies are turning on
and so it sort of hurts.

So now you are stepping into the next creator overlay; that is one that you have created consciously in order to interface with the human experience or whatever world of form you would be in. You would have to create a common overlay. This, as opposed the initial discussion of overlays, is done consciously by choice with direction and purpose where the other sort of ran based upon the patterns, the Energetic Fields of Influence, and habits.

And so now stepping into this creatorship creates a bit of a quandary for the ego personality because it can't decide which world it is in. "Am I in the human world where this means disease and illness or discomfort and pain? Am I in this world where I am a creator and I am actually creating something and this is done purposefully? Am I in the world where this is done purposefully?" So now it becomes a little confusing; and you flip back and forth because you are not quite detached from the unconscious overlays that you put on and you are starting to experience some of the creatorship that is available.

Sometimes we perceive change as discomfort.

So you are back and forth. "Oh this one hurts. This means discomfort. Oh this one hurts because I am morphing." As you start to make these shift and you flip flop back and forth, you may get nausea. As you flip flop back and forth in these overlays, it will affect almost like the equilibrium in the body. So you know when you spin on a ride and you get dizzy and you may get nausea and those types of the things? It will be a very similar thing. And so acclimating to that will take a little bit.

And it is good to understand this so that you don't go getting worried about, concerned about, frustrated with it. And, yes, accepting it is probably the only thing you can do while you are going through it because it is part of your expansion. And if you look at this and see this where you have come from, how you have walked your way from unconscious behaviors to understanding about your behaviors to understanding about beliefs, and then patterns, and then Energetic Fields of Influence, and then overlays and see how this progression is taking place and it has all prepared you to move to this next level as comfortably as possible.

Just imagine going from totally unconscious to this creator overlay snap, the ego personality would not be able to manage that great of a change. But look how it has taken place for you who have done your homework. It has taken place, oh, a little bit challenging but it has processed and progressed and it is almost what you would call natural.

And really this is simply an awakening process. You are awakening to the creator that you are. And the key to this now stepping into the creator is a remembering that you are not your behaviors; you are not your experiences. You are the experiencer of your experiences. You are the creator of those experiences also. And in creating those now in this conscious place, you can step out completely,

feel completely different, unique and new; create a conscious overlay in which to interact with other levels or realms of perception, in other words, other realities.

Those realities could be multiple just in the human world alone. It could be working with somebody who lives in the ghettos in the city to connecting with somebody who lives out in the woods, to somebody who is on a 'spiritual journey' or someone who is a scientist. Each one of those interactions will require an overlay in order to interact with them. So you, as the conscious creator, would create an overlay, place that over the situation so that there was an interface available between you and whoever or whatever you are wanting to connect with and experience.

Creators and Tolerance

Overlays at the creator level are tools to interface with other realities. When you are interacting with people in the average human reality, then your tolerance is required because while you are switching back and forth from unconscious overlay to conscious overlay, you are going to step into your patterns and your issues and whatever might be left. Your own frustration of this transitional process which can be at times a little frustrating because sometimes you are there and sometimes you are not; then you are there and then you are unexpectedly not; and this gets a little frustrating.

Overlays at the creator level are tools to interface with other realities.

So when you are interacting with others then you must be aware and more tolerant about what is going as to not unload your frustrations or even judgments on those you are interacting with. Because now that will bleed through the overlay and now that will create and you won't even know you have created. Then you will have people responding. And you may be even in a position of saying "Oh I didn't intend to do that; that is not what I meant; it is not what I wanted to do."

But do you know what? When you are a creator, one single thought creates. One single thought manifests. Thank god you had the grace of not manifesting instantly because imagine what your life would have been like with every thought that you had. It might not have been so fun.

So having tolerance with yourself in your process going back and forth while you are learning this new awareness and being able to travel consciously, having tolerance for others while they are not on that journey and you are having challenges with the journey, so that tolerance is very important for both yourself and others in whatever reality they may be in.

Add to the tolerance your tolerance of the sound and vibration of the density that you are leaving. Because as you are flipping back and forth from the conscious and unconscious overlays, when you are in the unconscious overlay and you are sort of semi-consciousness, you are still experiencing that reality in a more of a real way which makes it a little bit more intense, a little bit more unpleasant, a little bit more disruptive. That will also create a bit of a disturbance in your energy system.

And in all of this, there are a lot of little factors that are all piling up. Because of all of these little factors, don't be trying to limit it to one factor or two factors.

Understand that there are multiple aspects and you are learning to work through all of them. So that too would be being tolerant.

Understand that overlays can now be a tool when you are a creator. It is just like anything else that you have learned.

Any human experience is a skill and those skills can be used from a creator perspective. It will look the same but they will be from a different awareness. So just a reminder, overlays at the creator level are tools to interface with other realities.

The Cyber Space Overlay

The internet and computers, as much as everybody knows everything on there, is just a visual creation and even possibly doesn't even exists somewhere or may not be valid, this whole system is simply a metaphor for what you create as a human being. Everything you create in your 'real life.' is exactly the same illusion that you create in your computer life. The only difference is that people tend to believe their real life. And now many people, being addicted to the internet, are beginning to believe in the computer life. And it becomes a whole real world that they don't even
have to interact with their physical bodies.

Everything you create in your 'real life'
is exactly the same illusion
that you create in your computer life.

So the cyber world is really a world without form creating the illusion of form. So it is somewhere between the physical world and the spirit realm. And it is simply another illusionary metaphor for what you actually do in your physical life with your physical human body. It needs to be clear that what you can picture and visualize and see and hear on the internet or on your computer, everybody pretty much knows it's fake; it is an illusion; it is all optics. Well that is all your human life is except that it is not just visual optics; it is kinesthetic.

So we have another world of illusion that is just again another parallel to your human life. And it could be a place where someone could get lost. They could get lost in their video games; they could get lost in their 'You Tube.' They tend to get lost in their 'Facebook' or 'Pinterest' like it is some reality. People putting pictures up and typing silly statements about what they did today.

It is an absurd illusion and they use that to experience the world. It is not really an experience; it is an illusionary experience. It has no tactile sensation or experience to it. It is not to say that things can't be worked out and there aren't other things going on.

But theoretically, if we came to be in a physical body, why are we not having a physical experience? Why would we go into cyber space? Well, there is no need for a physical body to do that because if you just cross the other side of the veil and you leave your form, you can watch just like you are in cyber space. And you can see all kinds of lights and colors and things occurring and you don't have to manifest into a physical form.

It wasn't the purpose of manifesting in the physical form. But the cyber world gives you that opportunity if you establish your physical experience. And that is why you took the human body. Then you can actually use cyber space to sort of connect to the other side of the veil and understand how it works and get connected to that in-between world. In a way, cyber space is like an astral world. And you can connect to the other side while in your physical realm.

Well in a way, if they actually connect to the internet the way that they could, it could be a visual, telepathic experience through which you could interpret some things that were not able to be physically experienced through your human physical experience and then integrate as much of that you want into your kinesthetic, sensory, physical experience. So you could potentially have more experiences if it was used the proper way.

But the problem is, as we talked about you losing your consciousness, you could lose your consciousness to the cyber space and then believe in the cyber space. And now you have a double, double, double overlay. So you have multiple overlays in your human experience and you have multiple overlays of your cyber space experience which could be infinite.

So now you have all these coupled overlays and you could be completely disconnected from the spirit within. Or you could be conscious and observe all of this and play in all of those realms and have a greater experience.

Your Overlays Imprison and Energetically Limit You

When you recognize that your overlay onto other people is a subjective imprisonment of their nature, you have imprisoned them with your projection and overlay of a reality and therefore you cannot see them or their essence. They are subject to your constraint when they are in your energy field. When they leave you, they are freer, they are different people, they experience things differently and they do things differently and they don't have nearly the same experience that you have with them, because they are either subject to someone else's overlay, or they're free of overlays entirely or partially depending on their own consciousness.

When you have an overlay and you overlay that onto someone else, which is just simply a projection of a reality, when you have an overlay onto them imagine you are enveloping them energetically so therefore you can only see them the way that your overlay dictates they can be seen.

When you advance to another level of looking at your own stuff and realizing that you are the creator of your reality in totality, you can release them of your overlay and look at them through clarity and no overlay. When or if they feel that, they are freed to be something else, maybe not necessarily what you expect, what you anticipate or what you desire, but they are freed to be something else and therefore the relationship automatically changes without effort, because you have taken off the overlay or the imprisoned, subjective opinion you have of them or belief system and they are no longer layered with your junk.

They are freer to be themselves, whether they're in their own overlay or you get to see their essence, it doesn't matter. When you are unconditionally accepting, you are no longer placing overlays on anyone. That is required before you can unconditionally love. You cannot love an overlay because it's not real, because it is fake, because it is an image, it is a hologram. You cannot love a hologram because there is no essence in a hologram.

So we go back to the concepts, unconditional acceptance means you do not project overlays, you sit in neutrality, observing whatever anyone is in their essence, or whatever they are choosing to project for you to experience, that is unconditional acceptance, which makes the ability or the potential of unconditional love to exist.

When you are unconditionally accepting or without an overlay, you free the other person to be whoever it is they want to be, or want to experience, or that they truly are. You can't determine which one it is that they're going to present of those three options, but you get to experience whatever it is. When you can truly see and unconditionally love, you will see through their own overlays or projections and see their true essence, and one true essence seeing another true essence, is unconditional love, that is love at its essence. To repeat it, unconditional love, REAL LOVE, is when one essence, being, witnesses the essence of another being.

That's it, there is nothing else. There is no human emotion, there is no rushes of joy, there is no ecstatic pleasure, there is no sensuality, or sexuality involved. There is simply the witnessing of essence to essence, no personalities, no ego structure, no karma, no soul memory, no nothing, essence to essence experience that is REAL LOVE.

You must get past your overlays to even have the possibility of unconditional acceptance to even have the possibility of real love, and when you realize that you are creating those overlays or those subjective imprisonments energetically, you can choose to release them, or you can choose to sustain them. It's all up to you, but then that determines your experience of unconditional acceptance or real love.

None of them have to do with human connection, it is so far beyond that, that this is what the ancient ones could not describe nor was it translated accurately. Essence to essence witnessing and experiencing is the divine love.

So your overlays, your projections, separate you from the real love. You are the creator of your reality, in totality, period. When you recognize that, you have the option to become conscious, make a conscious choice, and experience unconditional love, but it's nothing like anyone has defined it as.

Everyone who has defined it has created an expectation which can never be fulfilled because it's all a belief system, which makes it another overlay, and another projection so therefore you cannot experience real love, or divine love, as long as you hold any belief about it, for an essence to essence witness and experience has no belief, has no overlay, has no expectation, it has nothing except the experience of essence experiencing essence. That is divine love.

Moving beyond your overlays, your belief systems, your core beliefs, etcetera, allow you to experience divine love. Again, we cannot reiterate enough times -- divine love is nothing like anyone has ever expected it to be. When you experience, there are no words for it, and the best words we can give you is an essence to essence experience, with no judgment which means no interpretation, a pure experience of essence. When one has experienced an essence to essence experience, then they recognize that all are from the same source. Essence is essence; although your individuated essence has a personality that is quite unique unto itself because of its own experiences within the universes or multiverses.

Anything other than that is a limited experience that is not divine love, and there are multitudes of levels, as there are multitudes of multiverses. In your experiences, understand that your overlays create your realities, imprison other people to be limited when they encounter you to your overlay. Sometimes they'll feel trapped, confined, restrained, or repulsed by that overlay. Some will embrace it because it fits the need for them to hide from their own essence, and many other reasons, but you are the creator of all that you experience.

It gives way to the irony that nothing is real, and everything is real, so nothing outside of you is real, but everything you experience about outside of you is real to you.

You created everything out there the way you experience it, others have done the same, so there is a lot of stuff floating around out there but it is all real, differently, to everyone and yet none of it out there is real. It is only real based upon the overlay that you have projected onto it. Since everyone has projected a different overlay, there are different realities for everyone, and yet the canvas is blank.

Everyone is only perceiving the canvas in the way that they want to, based upon their programming and their own personal illusion. The canvas is just a canvas. Yes, there are a bunch of individuals out there, there are separate appearing beings out there, but none of them are any way unless someone is perceiving them some way. They themselves perceive themselves a different way and that is a different reality than the way everyone else is perceiving them.

The irony is, nothing out there is real, and yet everything you experience about out there is real, but only from within you, hence the old phrase, everything is an illusion. It is an illusion because nothing is ultimately or absolutely real, it is only subjectively real. The only thing real is that there is a canvas out there, but what is on the canvas is an illusion based upon everyone's subjective reality or overlays.

The overlays are based upon all of your experiences or programs based upon your experiences. Therefore, you project onto the canvas, everything that exists on the canvas, and there are simply molds of individual beings, planets, places, animals, creatures, critters, that you are projecting onto as a reality. If you take away all of the overlays, nothing exists except essence. This is little cosmically mind boggling, so not everyone is going to be ready to hear this or even put that into play.

So break it down simply and say that all of your overlays create your reality, and your reality is yours alone, and as long as you believe or perceive what you believe or perceive then it is real to you, and it is unique unto you -- similar to others, but unique unto you.

Others that are similar enough will bond into a commonly perceived overlay, which allows for a collective existence, such as the planet Earth, such as the country of the United States, or England, or Germany, or Brazil. Those with a common bond have a common collective overlay, and a common experience, none of them makes them real or absolute truths, but they are truths unto the individual, and the commonly bonded overlay that we will call a reality. It's all made up by you or the collective you's.

Question your own reality to see what is real and what is your creation. By asking other people what they're doing and why they're doing it, you are questioning your own overlay. You are not questioning the person, and by assuming whatever they tell you is true, is to say that I am willing to listen your reality to question my own reality, to see if my overlays are something that I want to continue or not.

Do my overlays serve me? If they don't serve me, I get to eradicate them now because I've asked you what you're doing and why you're doing it to discover my own reality and my own overlays, not to question you as person because I can't do anything about you, and I don't even care about you in some way.

I am questioning my reality, that's why we have insisted that you question everything, not doubt, but question, to investigate your overlays, to investigate your own reality, to decide if you're finished with this reality or not. Are you ready to create a new one? Are you ready for another experience, or are you wanting to hang onto this one and suffer a little longer, have a little more pain, a little more trauma, a little bit more victimhood, whatever you're doing. Are you finished with it?

So it is about questioning your own reality and people misinterpret that. You're not questioning others like we're detective at a murder scene. We're questioning our own realities, we're asking others questions to find out if our overlays are accurate or they're something I'm finished with.

So, I am investigating my own truths, to discover what truths I want to play in at any given moment, and hopefully to discover my own absolute truth, to then decide what realities I want to play in, for me, not for anyone else, but for me. This is the purpose of question everything, because everything is your reality.

This is all about service to self; it's not about serving anyone. How you serve others incidentally is by serving self. When you serve self, with the broadening of or the expansion of your consciousness, you free them from your overlays, which allows them to be something different with you, when they interact with you, if they want to be something other than what they have been with you. If they don't, then they'll still play the way that they want to play, because they're not finished with their experience. But you have given them the opportunity to experience their interaction with you differently, by removing your overlay of them and you begin to remove the overlay by questioning everything for yourself to find your own transparency and freedom, which then automatically frees them.

That's why we say, the way to change the world is to change yourself because when you change your overlay of the world, you free the world to show up differently if it so chooses. When enough people do that individually, the whole world changes because everyone is free from the overlay that was common to everyone and therefore there can be a new reality experienced because everyone has set everyone free from the old reality, and there didn't need to be any protests or movements, because everyone was automatically freed from the overlay, because every individual freed themselves from the overlay, which released everyone from the subjective imprisonment they have placed on the entire planet, and thereby created freedom, consciously and with free will. Then they get to experience individual interaction free of overlays and everyone living their individualized truths without being limited or subject to a collective or individual overlay, imprisoning them and confining them, and limiting them to only certain behaviors and experiences and that is freedom for everyone.

When you ask questions, or when you question everything, if you question from a neutral space, from you questioning your own reality, you free everyone and yourself. But if you ask question through an overlay, you still imprison them based upon the overlay of questioning, because you are questioning their reality, them, their existence, based upon your overlay. That's completely different than questioning your own reality knowing that you're the creator of it, and neutrally asking the question so that you can self-discover.

The other way is discovering others so that you can explain your overlay. That's not a pure questioning, that is a conditional overlaid questioning, which is still imprisoning, so it looks the same, but the energy of it is completely different and therefore the outcome is completely different. Some will say it doesn't work because they're questioning through an overlay, rather than questioning their own reality, within themselves, without an overlay on others, completely different outcomes, completely different energies. Very few will get to that place.

Overlays - The Human Illusion

The human overlay is the illusion that you are human. It is the illusion created of/by beliefs, thoughts, knowings, attitudes. It is the veil of all of these things.

And we would speak of the veil as being a covering over your consciousness through which you see, believe, act and seem to understand that which you are interpreting through the colors or distortions of that veil.

The misunderstanding that you are human is one of those veils. The belief in that veil being accurate and true is the overlay in your experience which causes or triggers your response to what you are perceiving. The human overlay was necessary for you to have the experience that you have had. But this time has come to an end! It is time to see clearly without the veil.

The longer you remain in the human veiled overlay, the more difficult and challenging your life may seem to be. This veiled perception is limiting and finite, yet endlessly looping. This veiled overlay is imprisoning and designed to keep you limited. Only you can choose to see clearly and remove the veil or overlay and change the way you experience your human journey!

Many try to achieve this through spirituality....this is just an escape! There are many who say they know. There are many who teach how to do this. But there are only a handful who have achieved this mastery! There is no way to mastery except through experience!

The misunderstanding that you are human is the veil.

This overlay is no longer useful to you. It served a purpose; created an experience and an understanding of the human world the way it is at this moment and the way it was in what you would call the past. But the past is no longer true and this moment is now completely changed and different. It is time for you to remove the veil. Use the wisdom experienced that you have gained by having that veil. Remove the overlay.

There also has become a dependency on that overlay in order to identify and create an experience that you perceive you are having. This dependency is like an addiction because the fear of being without your substance, which is the overlay, creates such anxiety to the ego personality because it has been so out of touch with the direct contact of your Spirit. And by becoming more aware of your I AM presence, the direct contact becomes more common and there is no need for the overlay. The dependency on that overlay becomes dissolved.

Seek your spirit and that direct connection and the overlay will automatically be dissolved. In some ways, it is very easily done, effortlessly, without work, without concentration. There is no process. There is simply the process that you are going through anyway.

Seek your spirit and that direct connection and the overlay will automatically be dissolved.

This need and addiction to processes and techniques is part of the overlaid veil that keeps you trapped. If you truly understood that there was no process, no technique, nothing for you to actually do except be conscious, you would find that everything would dissipate very quickly. Again, the need for all of these processes, ideas, techniques, teachers, this is all part of the human overlay.

It is time for you to truly recognize that there are no teachers except yourself. There are those who tap you on the shoulder and awaken you to remember this truth; but that it is all there is. You are the teacher of Self. And in truth it is not actually a teaching; it is a remembrance or an awakening from your slumber of the imagined human overlay that you have become so accustomed to and dependent upon.

Your experience and your interactions with others does not depend on this overlay for you have already achieved the skills necessary to have those interactions. It is the overlay that creates your difficulties and challenges. It is not what keeps you comfortable and safe.

Be free. Truly free. Allow for your human overlay to dissolve. It is occurring. All you have to do is have that intent and allow yourself to have the experience that is about to come. In truth that which is about to come has already occurred and it is only that you are going to remember the experience that you have already had which allows you to be your Spirit in the human form without the human overlay.

Overlays -The Gathering Meditation

Center in the heart, take a couple of deep breaths.

Now we are going on a journey to collect our overlays. Now as you feel the connecting your heart center from there make the statement:

"I am the creator of all of my experiences and overlays and as the creator I now move forth to gather all of these experiences. I traveled the universes, the galaxies, the dimensions and all of existence gathering these overlays and experiences. As my purpose is to pull everything back to me and become the one I AM."

And from your heart chamber you will send multiple mini

pods of light in multiple directions through all of existence to gather your overlays. Launch your ships now in all directions and know that each ship will gather, find and return with the overlays that you have created through all experiences.

It will not be a burden; they will be light, they will be easy, they will be fluffy, they will enjoy coming back home. There is nothing heavy or dense, there was nothing that was troublesome or painful, in fact there will be great joy as they see the ships arriving to collect them, they will stand waiting to return and be beamed onto the ships because they know they are returning home and as all the multiple ships reach all of their multiple existences each one in their beam that they send to each overlay or experience communicates the love of your I AM presence, that you are returning home.

"We have finally come to get you. We know that you have waited and journeyed and you have longed for home, you have experimented and experienced all in the name of the love. We have come to get you. This is the great retrieval we call you all home."

You may see or feel multiple of these. We just feel the greatness of all of it occurring. This is the evacuation that they speak of, this is the ships coming to get them that they speak of but what no one knew was that you are the ship. Gather them all now and feel their joy of returning onto the ships on their way back to **you,** the heart, the mother ship.

Feel them all coming, all returning and just take a few moments to feel them all being beamed up, feel them all rejoicing, returning to the ship and the anticipation of returning home - everyone is called home now.
Feel them as they start to land in the mother ship; feel them enter the heart, the docking station. Feel them come in droves by the thousands, by the hundreds, by the millions from all over, from places you can't even begin to imagine, but you can feel from where there at, from where they have come, feel the wholeness as they return and feel their joy as they enter the heart as they dock within the mother ship - *you.* See them get out of the ships and within the heart they are coming to the great hall, they will all gather there. See them as the recognize each other as they in a split second share their experience and the joy of being reunited with each other as they enter the great hall.

The great hall is glorious! The great hall is beautiful, brilliantly lit, magnificently colored. When they enter the hall they float. There is no walking, there is no gravity, they direct wherever they go with intent. See them interact with each other and when you see them in the great hall you can actually see and feel them enter into one another because there are no physical boundaries, they pass through one another, they join together in larger orbs or bubbles as they merge.

And the great hall has a magnificently high ceiling, it's a magnificently high beautiful dome with a portal at the top leading out to just this brilliant white light and as the hall fills you feel the completeness within your heart knowing that all the overlays and experiential perceptions have returned, all of the emissaries you put out to the universes have returned. There is a wholeness that you may never have remembered experiencing and it is incredibly full and in the hall is huge and yet it doesn't feel crowded at all.

The last ships arrive, the last aspects and overlays enter the great hall and it is just this open hall and beings are floating in that hall. Some are on what some would perceive of as the ground, some are floating toward the ceiling and you see the orbs or bubbles joining and as all the individual orbs join you notice that they change colors every time another orb enters or departs. There are so many colors; there are more colors than you can imagine in shades that you have never seen before. Everyone is home.

Now you begin to hear a tone. Everyone feels the tone, they all begin to hover toward the middle, all the bubbles begin to connect. What you begin the recognize is that all the bubbles are one giant bubble, one giant orb, but yet when you look within the orb you can see all the individual orbs making up the one. And you feel the sounds echo within the orb and as the sounds travel each individual orb sparkles as the sound hits it.

It all feels as one and now the top of great hall begins to open and that beautiful white light is all that is seen. Crystal and sparkles descend in and around the bubble, the one orb and the whole orb turns crystalline sparkling white and begins to just float up and out through the top of the great hall.

As it floats out of the great hall you feel it arrive in your heart, you feel the fullness of your heart . Feel that in your heart, as it begins to expand around your body. Feel the unity in your own bubble as one space.

"I am one, the one I am, I AM that I AM, and I am the one."

Welcome!!!
Take a deep breath and be back in your body.
Welcome the new you!!!

Advanced Lessons in Overlays

Overlays, we have spoken of them in regard to your human behaviors and interactions. Now we move to a little bit larger picture of the overlays, understanding that being a human is an overlay of the Spirit. It is, in essence, a covering in order to have an experience at a lower, dimensional, vibrational frequency; simply meaning in order to be in the worlds of density there must be some sort of an overlay to be able to interact and have the full experience of being human.

This overlay is what forms what we might call amnesia. This amnesia allows you to interact as a human being in order to learn the experiences that human beings have. At one time without those overlays, you could not have a full and rich human experience and get the complete learning and wisdom. As we move into the next levels of existence, we would say to you that it is time for those overlays to become extremely thin. Thin in the sense that they are something that you can use and have a human experience without forgetting who you truly are.

As we move into the next levels of existence, we would say to you
that it is time for those overlays to become extremely thin.

As those of you who have already been born, as the word goes, on earth, you are undoing or thinning the veils. And as you thin the veils, your human may have some difficulties, challenges, fears or apprehensions because it has been so habitually in control of your experience and what was going on in your quote 'human life.'

For those coming, being born into this earth plane, the veil will already be thinned. They will already have the ability to connect with their True Self or their Inner Knowing much more quickly and easily. Although some form of overlay will be experienced in order to be able to be a human being, the ability for them to transform into their knowing will be much quicker, easier and simpler.

For those of you already born into the human form, your transition and change may take some time based upon your ego personality and its resistance or compliance to the wishes of your Spirit. As you develop your memory, or should we say as you recall as the veil thins, you will find things coming quickly and easier than previously in your life experience.

The difficulty in letting go of your human patterning is very common but one must not get lost in the human experience and those ways of thinking and being. You must be open and willing to make shifts quantumly beyond where you are currently aware of or maybe even comfortable with. If you are being stretched beyond your comfort zone, into greater awarenesses, this signifies that you are moving in the appropriate direction. Look closely at how you are seeing the world and your experiences.

If you are seeing them the same way you have in the past, then you are involved in your overlays. It is time for you to take conscious control and direction; step into your ego personality and begin to thin the veils of the overlays that separate you from your awareness of your True Self and keep you locked in limited consciousness. This overlay of the Spirit is the next level for you to remove if you will.

In truth it is not actually a removal; it is a thinning and a dissipation of a consciousness that you perceived to be true. It is time for you to take conscious direction and make the command:

I AM the Presence of truth, wisdom and the inner knowing of my Spirit.

I thin the veil of ignorance and limited consciousness.

I AM the Truth.

I AM that I AM.

Behold the Presence of my I AM that I AM.

I consciously dissolve the overlays of limitation.

I consciously dissolve the overlays of human.

All this occurs calmly, smoothly, easily and painlessly.

There is no need for traumatic events.

There is no need for trauma in this change whatsoever.

I experience the dissolution of these overlays

with comfort, ease, understanding and loving acceptance.

As I AM that I AM in wholeness, in clarity, in peace, and understanding.

I release and dissolve the veils of limitations and the overlays of human illusion.

So Be It and So It Is, as I remember I AM that I AM.

Thinning of the Veil

The overlay, if you recall, is like a veil. It is placed between or over your awareness of your Spirit and all that you know deeply within. As the thinning of the veil takes place, it is easier for you to see through it; it becomes more opaque or transparent.

As it becomes transparent, you begin to experience things that you always knew existed but did not necessarily have the conscious awareness of experiencing. For example, some things that might occur: the feeling light in your body as if you had no body yet being fully present; observing what is happening without actually being in it **conscious** yet being fully there for the experience.

*As the veil becomes transparent, you begin to
experience things
that you always knew existed
but did not necessarily have
the awareness of experiencing.*

You may begin to see things that you previously did not see with your eyes such as flashes of light, flickerings, movement out the corner of your eyes, shapes, forms, spots before your eyes. You may begin to sense an awareness of things around you that you cannot see with your eyes. If you have ever walked into the woods in the dark and felt things that maybe creeped you out or felt icky or scary, this would be a similar thing.

When you walk into the woods and it is dark, what happens is that your external senses are lessened until you adjust which allows for your internal senses to become more heightened temporarily. But out of fear, typically, the average person will try to get sensed and oriented to their physical surroundings because they often become fearful.

And we would say to you, that those senses are picking up on the beings or entities that are just on the other side of the veil that with the human illusion and that overlay seem so very far away. But when that overlay is thinned or temporarily disconnected, you begin to feel and sense things that are not or were not there a moment ago when you were aware of your external senses.

These are all momentary glimpses of the thinning of the veil or the thinning of the overlay. These overlays again were created purposefully in order to allow you to fully have the human experience. Without these overlays, you would not be able to experience human emotion, human love, human fear, sensory experiences that can only be experienced very physically. So the veils, or the overlays, served a great purpose.

But as you advance or, should we say, expand your consciousness, the overlays become thinner. And that which you always knew but had forgotten while you were under the blanket of the human overlay, starts to come to light and you become aware of these things. You may feel things on your skin. In most cases it is not a physical touch of the skin; it is an energetic contact with your own energy field translated to your physical skin. As your physical skin is actually an energetic overlay or construct, the energetic contact or connection with, we will call it, the invisible on the other side of the overlay is sometimes felt physically. So remember there will be a lot of unique, yet known, experiences.

As you expand your consciousness, the overlays become thinner.
And that which you always knew but had forgotten while you were under the blanket of the human overlay, starts to come to light and you become aware of these things.

And the most difficult part of the thinning of the human overlay is that the ego-personality often kicks into fear because it does not recognize it or has not been acclimated to those experiences. But know that once you become used to these experiences and acclimate to these sensory awarenesses as well as new sight, both with the eyes and without the eyes, the fear will begin to dissipate.

And it is suggested that you speak to your human ego personality and console it like you would a young child. "It is okay. We are simply re-experiencing that which we already know. I am your Spirit and I speak to you with loving kindness and say to you, 'We are learning to grow together. As you expand, so does my experience. And as my experience and yours expand, we merge into one experience. You will slowly adjust, and I will be here to comfort you, to guide you, instruct you and answer your questions. As we experience and remember together, everything will be okay. That which you saw as a truth and an only existence you will see differently, you will begin to realize what we already know. And as we already know it, we will assist and comfort you in your transition as you give us the experience of having a human overlay and full, rich, human experience."

So as you merge together your human experience and your Spirit, the veil becomes thinner and the human experience becomes richer. It is seen in a new way without emotions from the human way but with an experience of, it is hard to find a word, but we would say an experience of, enjoyment. And we would want to say joy but most people perceived joy as 'exciting and yippee, yahoo,' and it is not quite that kind of 'joy.' It is like 'Wow, this is cool! We are having this experience and our wisdom at the same time. It all becomes one. This is such is new way to experience this human existence."'

So welcome the thinning of the overlay, the release of illusion. And at one time, we had also referred to this as freedom from limitations. Enjoy your new experience. Fear not as your greater wisdom will guide you. You need no one. You need only to remember and allow the integration of all of you into one experience.

Journal to Self-Discovery Pages

Energetic Overlays – Relationships and Communication

Who do you have problems communicating with? Do you put up a wall (overlay) first or do they?

Observe and write where you put up a wall (overlay) in a conversation or want to manipulate the conversation to get a certain outcome. Where do you have an emotional response?

Notice and write where you feel the person you are talking to is doing any of the above.

Energetic Overlays – The Communicator

Practice what you've read in section 3. How does it change your experience?

Overlays – Yours, Mine and Theirs

Where are you more invested in having people see it your way rather than openly hearing the other person or people?

Write a list of where you can see you put overlays on people, places and activities.

Overlays – Past and Present

If someone you are with is upset or having an emotional reaction observe if you take on the same emotion or if you feel responsible to change it. If either of these are true, this is your overlay. Write about the beliefs involved.

Patterning Explained

In what situations do you tend to lose consciousness and identify with the overlay?

What overlays can you see that you can just release?

Creators and Tolerance

Where do you get impatient, unload your frustrations and judgments on those you interact with or yourself? What do you need to do to change this process?

The Cyber Space Overlay

Where do you get lost on the internet? Where does it metaphor your human life?

How could you use it and play to have a greater experience?

Your Overlays Imprison and Energetically Limit You

Are you beginning to observe others without your overlays? How do they appear different to you?

When you ask others what they are doing or saying is it different than what you originally perceived? Can you see your overlay?

Are you ready to give up your overlays or are they still serving you somewhere?

Overlays – The Human Illusion

What processes and techniques are you still addicted to?

Advanced Lessons in Overlays

What fears, difficulties or challenges are you having in giving up your overlays?

Are you still seeing the world in the same way as you did in the past? If so, what do you need to do to take conscious control and direction?

Thinning of the Veil

Is or how are your experiences changing as the veil thins?

What are you sensing that you may not have sensed before (this may be subtle so take time to explore this)?

Notes

End

This book is designed to stimulate you to find your own answers within and to give you some guidelines, parameters and tools to assist you on your journey. No book, workshop, audio, web-site, course or lecture will ever be enough on its own to give you the answers. Your answers must be found and remembered by you; it is the only way that they become yours. If you depend on the answers from anyone else it is simply you repeating another's answers and discoveries. The best you can hope for is information that will give you guidelines and direction for your own inner memory and discovery of your own answers.

The intent of these books is to provide you with stimulating information and accurate wisdom that will assist each reader in finding their own answers, wherever they may lie or whatever they may look like. As with any other information, it is up to you to use and understand the materials, then discern how you can use it to improve your life.

For best results with this or any book we have published, read the information, understand it, feel it in your heart, then discern what resonates with you and is useful for your journey.

There is a meditative audio called "Beliefs a Higher Perspective" that goes with the last
copy email admin@itstimetoawaken.com

About the Author

Michael Cavallaro's life work has been finding ways for people to integrate their spiritual nature with their everyday lives. For almost 40 years, through classes, workshops, lectures, books, audios, articles and private consultations he has helped thousands of people lead healthier, happier lives by finding practical solutions to various challenges.

His training as a family intervention counselor and clinical hypnotherapist has given him insight into established approaches to problems. The exploration of a variety of spiritual practices, traditional and non-traditional methods, combined with his own experience and insights inspired him to integrate and apply ancient wisdom with modern life.

Michael's background is as varied as his interests. He has worked in the fields of construction, management, finance, insurance and more; taught in schools and prisons and currently teaches classes in artistic expression. He serves as an Educational Consultant for Teamwork Wins, Ltd, a non-profit organization that guides individuals with Invisible Challenges™ in becoming self-directed, free-thinking, creative individuals. Artistically, Michael has recorded several music CDs and creates unique, energy filled artwork. All these interests are brought together with the intent of bringing light to the world and assisting others in finding joy in their existence and the connection to their own true selves.

Though he is an international speaker, his true gifts stand out most powerfully in intimate workshops and individual sessions. Here Michael's ability to see clearly past the facades and into the ways humans block and defend themselves with their fears, shames and beliefs truly come out. His way of expressing what each person knows within their own heart but never fully admits allows participants the opportunity to shed what's not working in their life and let their own light shine. Michael lives in Pennsylvania with his wife Adele and is the founder of Living Concepts, LLC.

Michael Cavallaro is available for speaking engagements and private consultations.

For further information, free articles, audios, videos and blog or to find out more about classes, products, are working with Michael or a trained facilitator please contact us at:

admin@itstimetoawaken.com
Call 215-272-3153
or
visit our website: www.itstimetoawaken.com

Other Books by Michael Cavallaro
The 55 Concepts, A Guide to Conscious Living
Seven Steps to Freedom
Human Mastery Volume 1 & 2
Ramblings
Change Your Mind, Not Your Child
Loving Yourself

By Adele Saccarelli Cavallaro and Michael Cavallaro
Searching for Oz
Searching for Oz – The Journey Home : A Guide to Your Own Answers

See the website for additional products as well as classes and a free newsletter. After having read this book you now have all the information of how beliefs, patterns and programs work that you will ever need. To benefit from this you must find ways to apply this info or receive further education from www.itstimetoawaken.com or www.adeleandmichael.com

Made in the USA
Middletown, DE
09 September 2021